WALKER'S GUIDE

Hadrian's Coastal Route

Ravenglass
to Bowness-on-Solway

CLIFFORD JONES

D1422055

TEMPUS

MAIN ROUTE MAP

First published 2008

Cirencester Road, Chalford,
Stroud, Gloucestershire, GL6 8PE
www.thehistorypress.co.uk

Tempus Publishing is an imprint of The History Press

British Library Cataloguing in Publication Data.
A catalogue record for this book is available from the British Library.

ISBN 978 0 7524 4610 3

Typesetting and origination by The History Press
Printed and bound in the UK by Ashford Colour Press Ltd, Gosport, Hants

Contents

Introduction

The Western Hadrianic Frontier of the Roman Empire is little known by the general public. Until recently, the frontier was viewed as merely a series of forts, with a fluid means of defence and administration between them. The public was understandably drawn to the physical remains of a wall crossing from Bowness-on-Solway to Wallsend.

Archaeologists have always known different and it is only now that we are beginning to shout from the rooftops that the Western Frontier is as important as the stones that cross the Pennines.

Fortunately, through the efforts of a very small band of archaeologists and Hadrian's Wall Heritage Ltd, that position is changing. There is a wealth of magnificent and diverse scenery and amazing archaeology which rivals the sites along the better-known Hadrian's Wall.

Walking the frontier offers opportunities for personal adventure and discovery. It is not a single line to follow; the diversions are part of the whole. You can do all or some; there is plenty of variety in the West. Catch a train, or bus; buy local produce; enjoy a beer and a good bed. But most of all, enjoy the quest!

This guide offers the walker an insight into this relatively unknown world; the importance here is that history is still being revealed, and archaeologists are just starting the long process of understanding how the Western Frontier works.

Be part of history. Walk it!

Walking in the Roman Army's Footsteps

BASIC PRINCIPLES

Good, worn-in boots

To enjoy a good walk, have the right boots; this is a long-distance expedition capable of filling approximately ten days and a comfortable pair of boots is essential. So be prepared.

> *The Roman equivalent of our lightweight walking shoe or boot was the 'Caligae', an apparently flimsy leather sandal, not offering much in the way of protection from the elements, but at least it was well ventilated. A well-ventilated foot is a happy foot! Fitted with studs for grip and useful for imposing severe injury on fallen enemy forces and trampling new road surfaces alike, it was much tougher than it looked.*

Waterproofs

West Cumbria can be a glorious spot on a good day, but the weather can be extremely inclement, especially on exposed sections such as beaches or clifftops. A good quality set of lightweight waterproofs, including overtrousers, is a must.

> *The Roman equivalent was the 'sagum'. Winter conditions in the far north of Britain, especially with the need to stand still and observe rather than march about, led to the use of a thick woollen cloak, copied from the natives. The Vindolanda tablets identify a pressing and constant need for more socks and underwear, suggesting a cold posting. Also a smelly one!*

Bait: an army marches on its stomach

The route has mixed opportunities for provisioning, especially beyond Allonby if taking the Roman shortcut, and Silloth-on-Solway if on the main route. The author suggests that the walker carries adequate basic supplies to get them through at least a full day. Major opportunities to stock up are available at Seascale, St Bees, Whitehaven, Workington, Maryport and Silloth-on-Solway, but there are useful small shops throughout the journey which the author encourages the walker to use whenever possible.

The Romans set up milecastles as part of a defensive strategy, but also because the army understood that the men needed to rest at regular intervals; the walker should take note of this. The watchtowers were manned to keep a roving eye on the landscape and the walker should do too.

The Roman military understood dry rations, but when in a fort or on frontier duty the basic healthy diet would be a grain ration of 830g per day, issued as grain as it does not deteriorate like flour. Soldiers ground the grain themselves. Bread ovens are prevalent all over Roman military establishments, often used to keep parts of forts warm in winter. At Housesteads there are bread ovens near the latrines, useful to stop the occupants freezing in winter! Archaeological remains show that the troops had frying pans, allowing for a quick and easy meal in the field, and stew pots, producing a meaty dinner. Fresh vegetables complemented this diet and the soldier could further supplement this by popping into the local vicus (a civilian settlement, often for retired soldiers and craftspeople) to one of the bars or shops there.

Observe and record

As the author stresses, you, the walker, may notice something that he and his fellow archaeologists have missed. The idea of this guide is for the walker to explore and not be fooled by us so-called specialists and experts. Take a photo, make a note and let me know.

Here is a translated Roman intelligence report found at Vindolanda from the late first or early second century:

... the Britons are unprotected by armour (?). There are very many cavalry. The cavalry do not use swords nor do the wretched Britons mount in order to throw javelins.

British Museum P&EE 1986 10-1 34,
Room 49: Roman Britain

Common sense

Please keep to paths to keep erosion down and remember that agriculture plays an enormous part in the Cumbrian economy, so close gates after you. Plan ahead – ring establishments to check opening times.

Open mind

The walk deliberately starts at Ravenglass. It is good to start a walk involving Roman Britain with some physical remains (like the Roman Bath House) to encourage the walker, because it is followed by a virtual desert of obvious Roman remains for many miles. Slowly, as the walker progresses along the way, the process of observing and understanding the landscape begins.

A rise in the ground level, a river to cross, a change in the coastline, an old beach inland, a dried-up river course, all may be considered as indicators to the former landscape.

Why is that field that shape?
Why is that grass greener and longer than the rest?
Why does that crop not grow so well just in that one patch?

These are all clues which the walker can consider, record and enjoy the process of finding.

Wherever practicable, the walker is walking in the Roman Army's footsteps. A long-lost frontier, which through the walking, will come back to life.

In every case of a newly found site under archaeological research the exact location has been excluded from this guide. This is to protect the archaeology from those seeking only personal material profit. Please report any obvious human intervention or finds found as the result of erosion at known archaeological sites to:

English Heritage
North West Region
Canada House
3 Chepstow Street
Manchester, M1 5FW
Telephone: 0161 242 1400

Where possible provide details of location, including grid reference.

A Western Frontier

From a modern perspective, the heritage of the Western Frontier has been managed as a series of islands of interest down the West Cumbrian coast.

Ravenglass Fort and Bath House
Moresby Fort
Burrow Walls Fort
Maryport Fort and Environs
Allonby Bay Mileforts & Towers
Bowness-on-Solway Fort

The word 'frontier' is rarely used regarding the Cumbrian coast, but seems appropriate in the very straightforward sense of the coast being a geophysical line between land versus sea. So, a frontier it is!

A frontier suggests a need for a barrier, but it seems not to be a feature of the early advancement of Rome in the North West, and there appears to be no evidence of native coastal defences to stop the Romans arriving by sea. The Hadrianic constructions (AD 122) seem to be the most likely date for the works down the coast as well. There is no point in a barrier unless you protect the ends, otherwise people will just go around it!

The reader must consider that the Solway and the Cumbrian coast is a highway and it would be difficult, if not impossible, to stop every vessel from plying these waters, and so ideas travel as well as goods. The limitations of a frontier are apparent, as information and learning are universal; the Cumbrian coast would likely always have been a hotbed of political change.

Forts at key strategic river and coastal locations have more to do with the culmination of good long-term planning, exploiting the well-established trading links to maintain control of that trade, rather than the prospect of an invasion.

The Roman fleet, the packhorse of the Roman Army, required drinking water. Pure sources were required to keep the sea lanes open and the numbers of wells at Ravenglass are testament to this theory, and the pattern is repeated throughout the early coastal military establishments – good water close to the sea.

Once the Romans were fully established, fort locations offered the opportunity to tax vessels as they passed by. The Roman Empire relied on an efficient taxation system to maintain the status quo.

The list of heritage sites mentioned above is only a fraction of the likely actual material remains.

The walker can pose the question:

If the physical remains of Roman coastal watchtowers, mileforts and palisade ditches are traceable from Bowness-on-Solway to Maryport, does the system reach all the way to Ravenglass?

The answer is, quite probably, yes.

The reasoning is, if the contrary presumption is considered, that there is only a need for a physical 'side' to Hadrian's Wall to protect against an attack between Bowness-on-Solway and Maryport. This would expose Workington and its river, which offers potential for deep incursion into the hinterland.

It is very unlikely that the low-lying ground from Maryport to Workington was left so exposed, with only the fort at Burrow Walls to stop incursions.

There seems to have been a need to be seen to be administering a system of control, rather than to be constantly patrolling the coast, suggesting that there were only occasional forays from tribes outside the Empire attempting to exploit its wealth.

WHY STOP AT RAVENGLASS?

Whilst there is an apparently excellent means for an army to get inland via the River Esk, going further east than Hardknott would be impossible and the terrain to the north has limited routes via the Fells, all of which would be death traps. If an army attempted to turn immediately north after landing along the coastal strip, this would be met with opposition at Ravenglass and Moresby: the Fells are too rugged for a military force to pass unopposed, unlike the scenario at Workington, where the terrain is much gentler.

Active archaeological research between Ravenglass and Maryport continues apace to confirm a physical frontier. A hopeful sign is the recently reported discovery of a very deep ditch 'with wood at the bottom' running between Saltcoats and Drigg.

A THEORETICAL (BUT HOPEFULLY PLAUSIBLE) SCENARIO FOR ROMAN ARRIVAL

Imagine the scene during the last days of the Roman Republic. Marcus Tullius Cicero is busy prosecuting in Rome; meanwhile, the tide is lapping at a small trading vessel's bow as it arrives at the quiet native harbour of Ravenglass in the far-off land of mists beyond Gaul.

The beach is a No Man's Land; no one can truly call it their own, so trade takes place on this margin. Nobody feels as if they are being invaded when the sea reclaims it and all parties can put distance between each other quickly. There is nowhere to hide, so it is a place to meet strangers.

As long as no sword is drawn all is well, and this is the case as the parties greet each other with a mutual interest in commerce. The trader soon learns of good water sources, mineral wealth, what crops are grown, who is in command and who the natives' enemies are.

This process is repeated time and time again, and eventually a series of trading bases are set up with trustworthy local chiefs easily pacified by quality Roman products, such as good wine.

The trader's profitable return to his home base in Gaul creates interest from his fellow traders and this commercial inquisitiveness encourages others to consider exploration and exploitation. From Gaul, the trader's findings eventually reaches Rome; aristocrats, already accomplished at doing business with barbarians, are well-placed to consider investment in further expeditions into the far North West, and to protect their interests they provide traders with mercenary forces.

Back in Ravenglass, cordial relations continue between the natives and the trader and his compatriots; time passes and the next generation of the trader's family continue the cycle. Sailors and traders have further cordial relations with the native women and the social control of the native settlement begins the process of Romanization. Trade prospers, the knowledge and skills of some of the natives increase, and the enslavement of other groups is a profitable occupation, allowing for even more good living.

Such profit requires protection and the traders (for more have arrived) are allowed to construct suitable secure enclosures for their goods. The locals allow access to the hinterland; the source of the local wealth, be it agriculture, minerals or a mixture of both, is now open for thorough exploitation.

Time passes, as it tends to do. The Republic falls, the Imperial Age arrives, and the Emperor Claudius, needing to legitimise his control of the Empire (having removed his predecessor Caligula) by gaining a swift and effective victory over something and someone, and urged on by his tradesman friends eager to get into a market that had previously been the sole realm of aristocrats, stamps his mark by doing so in AD 43.

With Rome firmly established in Britannia, the gates for trade were thrown open and information, previously in the hands of the few, are suddenly available to the many. It is boom time, but after boom comes bust and the local chieftains found themselves in severe financial difficulty. They attempted to throw the Romans out and nearly succeeded, resulting in a heavy Roman military presence and a desire to control all parts of the island to prevent further revolt.

As a result of several generations of trading contacts, the increase in official military activity in the north of Britannia meant that the contacts to date were seen as valuable military intelligence. A wider understanding of the territory and peoples is crucial information for Gnaeus Julius Agricola, based at Chester, preparing for military forays into the far north.

A picture of the wealth of an entire region, its geography and demography was easily established; the allegiances and enemies known. All this makes a military occupation so much easier. A small fortlet was set up close to the harbour facility at Ravenglass – the Romans had arrived.

Such measures were undertaken without revolt, as many of the locals were very compliant; firstly, because they liked the Romans and the fine goods, and secondly, because the superior tribe of the region, the Brigante, were in the middle of a civil war against their own leaders, and it was deemed extremely useful to have a superior military force's protection.

This was a situation which exacerbated the fall of the strategic border capital, Carlisle, into Roman hands very early in the Roman military campaigns – led by Quintus Petilius Cerealis, who was in command of a vexillation of Legio IX Hispana in advance of Agricola's seaborne campaign.

Thus the Carvetii, the tribe of Ravenglass, and the western coast slipped neatly behind the protective shield of Rome, and small forts were erected to protect the interests and freedoms of all who would comply with Roman rule.

The traders acted in their own interests and those of Rome; they were unofficial 'Exploratio', scouts looking round the nearby headland for the next opportunity to trade. Such trade would continue to flourish even after the end of the Roman Empire; things may have become more complex and violent, but the profit margin was worth the risk. Ravenglass remained a port until Whitehaven became an easier beach to reach, as the coastline around Ravenglass began to make access more difficult.

Thus trade won the West!

AN ACADEMIC NOTE

The historians amongst you will no doubt be aware that Marcus Tullius Cicero was busy prosecuting Gaius Verres in 70BC. Verres, the former governor of Sicily, had stripped it bare not only of its treasures, but more importantly of its grain, so as to directly influence the Roman economy which relied upon Sicily as a breadbasket at that time. It should be stressed that Verres was not the only individual making fortunes in this way – he simply overstepped the mark.

On one hand, such activity was causing traders to look outside the Mediterranean. On the other, Cicero, a worthy historian, was aware that Sicily had previously been part of the great trading empire of Phoenicia, and that the Phoenicians traded with a far-off land for tin and other minerals, beyond the Pillars of Hercules, out into the Atlantic, beyond Roman control. Scholars had always known of this island. Herodotus, in 445BC, clearly identified the source of tin, as did Polybius in 120BC. So, Cicero alluded not only to the fact that Verres was stripping Sicily bare, but also to the well-established historical Sicilian links with places outside the empire, and that he was constructing craft specifically to go there.

If traders and ships' captains knew the way to Cornwall, it is not a great leap of imagination to consider they might have found Cumbria without too much trouble.

THE CUMBRIAN COAST: A BRIEF HISTORICAL GUIDE

Like any part of Great Britain, the fact that Cumbria is on an island means that the coast played an enormous part in the development of the hinterland. The sea, estuaries and rivers are a highway and ever since man worked out that wood floats, the opportunity to travel round the next bend by means of floating rather walking would have appealed.

Archaeology gives us a graphic picture of coastal living 6,000 years ago at Waberthwaite, on the south side of the River Esk, with evidence of hearths and shelters showing a community taking advantage of the river and sea. The evidence offers physical examples of exchange, trade with other communities, suggesting a sophisticated understanding of place, territory and value.

There are equally interesting remains of early coastal living at St Bees, on the landward side of the then-island with Mesolithic flint scatters.

The wheel came late to parts of Cumbria because the road system was involved in a great deal of 'up' and 'down' on paths no wider than a mule. Sleds proved more successful in much of the terrain. The coast road was the beach and, until the coming of the railway, coastal trading vessels would be venturing into every estuary, bay and harbour on a regular basis to trade with the locals.

Exports from Cumbria are notable in the fact that they are dominated by iron and coal, but there is evidence of the transportation of pottery, tiles, bricks, wool, stone and finished iron goods, such as shovels and, latterly, rail and heavy machinery.

The rail and the steam engine led to the death of coastal trading; the ease and regularity of service (not relying on the tide) and the physical building of the line along the coast firmly sealed off many age-old coastal routes forever.

All this activity creates a heavy industrial base, but the visitor often thinks this is merely located in places such a Whitehaven or Workington – it is not. Picturesque Eskdale was a thriving industrial powerhouse in Roman times and continued to produce iron into the late eighteenth century. With the forestry being managed for coppice wood, the charcoal was transported to other sites to maintain production demands. Ore mining was the reason that the 3ft gauge at Ravenglass and Eskdale was constructed. Notably, the ore was transferred at Ravenglass to railway wagons on the standard gauge Furness railway, not to coastal vessels (although a branch was planned). The days of trading by sea was at an end by the 1870s. The pleasant scenery and quaintness of the landscape belies the past.

Being beside the seaside is good for you; the bracing air certainly does clear the cobwebs, and the development of Seascale as a holiday resort from the 1850s onwards indicates a confidence in the future and wealth. From the 1700s onwards, strategic locations where coal could be exported or used for the production of iron goods, developed into industrial powerhouses such as Barrow in Furness, Millom, Whitehaven and Workington. This created wealth, poverty, smoke, smell and noise. Seascale is the result of the need to escape these realities; for those who could afford to do so, grand houses were available for rent which overlooked the beach from the aptly named Banks, and for those with less in the pocket, a day trip courtesy of the Furness Railway would fit the bill. Grand expansion plans collapsed with the First World War and echoed the slow decline of West Cumbria, a slide that went into freefall in the 1930s, only recovering briefly in the Second World War when the need for steel was at its greatest.

A remote location, an available workforce and an urgent need to maintain a standing in the world led to the Nuclear Age landing on the Cumbrian coast on two ex-MOD sites. Seascale, being close to both, suddenly took on a new life that reflected the way West Cumbria would be for the next sixty years.

Atomic technology replaced the coal industry; steel was finally 'corporately refocused' to Scunthorpe, leaving a large hole in the focus of Workington, but one that it is doing its very best to fill as West Cumbria has a nuclear future – the work at Sellafield is not a five-minute job and the waste material from powering a nation does not just go away.

Balancing that undoubted expertise with tourism and community regeneration is a long haul for all involved. There is a genuine attempt to open up the West to wider investment in the future, and your walking of the Frontier is part of it. This is a journey of discovery in more ways than one.

There is as much of the Western Frontier left as there is of Hadrian's Wall. You just can't see it yet.

Getting Started

The walker will find most of the route relatively easy going under foot; much is on well-maintained tracks or minor roads. Sign posts are, for the most part, very helpful, but the walk does not follow the Hadrianic Cycle Route 72 religiously. The walker can visit places the cyclist cannot.

Remember to close gates behind you and greet people with a smile because Cumbrians will talk to you. This behaviour may seem a little strange to the more reserved, but is quite normal and you may find it is catching.

You can start this journey at virtually any point, because the Network Rail route from Carlisle to Barrow in Furness is a coastal railway; the exception being the stretch from Maryport to Bowness-on-Solway, but there are bus services that fill the gap or of course you could walk!

For the purpose of this guide we will be walking from Ravenglass to Bowness-on-Solway, simply because that is the way the author decided to walk it.

Take a map, though not, primarily, to prevent you getting lost. Treat it as an adventure; there is much to explore and understand. There are stretches where the walker should think twice and take considerable care, obviously with main roads, sections of cliff walking and river and stream fording; you are a stranger in a strange land, and you will not know the territory well; use your natural inner caution as your guide.

Please remember that you are in Cumbria; the infrastructure is a tad on the thin side. The railway between Whitehaven and Barrow in Furness does not currently operate on Sundays. Buses operate, but often sporadically in the rural areas, and bus stops are likewise only known to the locals. Taxi services are available in larger communities.

Train operators, bus services, hotels and pubs are listed with telephone numbers. A really useful tool is 'Cumbria & North-East Journeyplanner', available on your PDA.

ROUTE PLANNING

The walker may wish to dip in and out of this guide for weekend excursions; here are some basic facts to note. Remember that the details will change so check with service providers and the Journeyplanner website or phone on **0871 200 22 33.**

Rail:

Ravenglass to Carlisle, Monday to Saturday.
Carlisle to Whitehaven, every day (limited Sunday).
Carlisle, Workington, Whitehaven and Barrow in Furness have booking offices; elsewhere please pay on the train. Services are operated by Northern Rail.

Bus:

Carlisle to Whitehaven, daily (limited Sunday).
Carlisle to Ravenglass, one connecting service down coast, two back (requires changes).
Whitehaven to Ravenglass, Sundays (surprisingly useful).

traveline

Maryport to Silloth-on-Solway, Monday to Saturday.
Carlisle to Bowness-on-Solway, daily (limited Sunday).

http://www.traveline.info/index.htm
Keywords: Traveline, Cumbria

DO CHECK IN ADVANCE REGARDING ALL SERVICES AND FACILITIES

Please Note:
Bus stops are an uncommon sight in many areas. Take local advice, and normally in very rural areas the bus will stop where it is safe to do so, if a clear hand signal is given.

WHERE TO STAY:

This guide is separated into days, all ending at points where there are accommodation options. But remember to book in advance, and that further north on the route, the options become scarcer, so good planning is a must.

Those taking their home in their pack, please ask before you pitch if not using recognised sites.

STARTING THE WALK AT RAVENGLASS:

The best way to arrive at Ravenglass is by rail, either down the coast from Carlisle, or up from Lancaster via Barrow in Furness. In both cases, the traveller will gain the sense of scale; West Cumbria is a long way from anywhere. That is what makes it unique. If arriving on Sunday, the bus from Whitehaven is an equally great experience.

Arriving at Ravenglass, you will be instantly aware that the station is also the pub. The Ratty Arms is named after the Ravenglass & Eskdale Railway, the terminus of which is right next door to the modern line. The Lal Ratty was built to convey haematite for the iron-producing furnaces that flourished along the Cumbrian coast in the late nineteenth century; now, it provides a regular service that allows the explorer to visit Eskdale.

The village itself has a pretty main street, with pinch points at ether end to hold cattle and sheep before being transhipped onto vessels. Ravenglass was a port long before the Romans and remained in constant use until the eighteenth century, and this has left its mark. The main street, with its cottages so close to the River Mite and the convergence with the Rivers Irt and Esk, is a potentially perilous location for living. But when the nearby Muncaster Castle decided to tidy up its immediate environs, the dwellings of the locals living near the castle were demolished and, not wanting to waste good agricultural land, the shore was the answer for these outcasts.

There are indications of massive sawn oak timbers beneath the buildings and street, suggesting that the street started life as a purpose-built hard for beaching vessels. The construction was to prevent erosion by the River Mite or the sea.

Many historians suggest Ravenglass was chosen as a port because of the convergence of three rivers. This is not the case; the River Irt only turned towards Ravenglass in relatively recent times, and the original course of the Esk likewise suggests that only the Mite provided a sufficient depth of water for large sea vessels in Ravenglass at the time of the Romans.

The main points of interest in Ravenglass are the substantial remains of the Roman Bath House and the fort site. Follow the signs from the village centre marked Bath House. These remains are quite obvious; what is not is the vicus, the large civilian settlement attached to the fort and port, which lies silently beneath the fields along the way to and by the Bath House.

The Bath House remained because it was a relatively small, well-built building that could be defended. After the demise of Roman control, the drastically changing world meant that coastal locations were profitable but dangerous places to be, and the thick walls of the Bath House, having once supported a vaulted roof, provided excellent foundations for a stronghold.

The fort, cut through by the building of the railway, lies next to the Bath House. The map at the site is very useful and the fort is quite clear to the eye as a series of mounds with a regular enclosing ditch. However, the part of the fort on the west side of the railway line, accessed by the lane that passes Walls Mansion to the right, is a very sad site; it is eroding away into the sea at an alarming rate. Excavated on this eroded edge in the 1970s, the evidence showed that there had been a fortlet on the site from the second century and a fort on the site until the fifth century. It saw continuous use throughout the Roman occupation of the North.

It seems traditional to get one's boots wet at the start of a walk, and there is no better place than by these fallen stones. If the tide is out the walker can walk back to Ravenglass along the beach or via the path accessed by the volunteer-built steps onto the headland, where a wonderful view of the estuary can be gleamed.

Throughout this adventure the walker will need to have a good sense of imagination. Remains above the ground are few and far between. The remains are there, we just haven't got round to digging them up yet.

Let us be frank. The more people that walk this route, the more likely that regional development agencies and central Government will offer funds to us archaeologists to carry out serious research; up until now, that funding has not been there. For the last twenty-two years the author has been undertaking research between Cockermouth and Ravenglass, and can think of seven archaeological digs involving Roman sites that have taken place in all that time. Excavating is not the entire picture; there has been considerable background research and the opportunity to excavate as a result is now mounting up. With your help, buying this guide and walking the land, much more will be done to fill the gaps in our knowledge of this frontier.

Hadrian's Wall has had over 200 years of serious research, the Western Frontier barely seventy, save for Maryport, where research goes back to the seventeenth century. As far as we can gather, the Western Frontier never needed a stone wall, but a substantial vallum and palisade was constructed, including frequent watchtowers and mileforts with well-manned bases from which to administer the hinterland and, as the Roman world began to change, to protect the coast from attack.

No doubt next week someone will come across a substantial stone wall, just to prove us all wrong!

AN EXCURSION:
TO HARDKNOTT BY TRAIN

The walker deciding to venture to the Roman fort at Hardknott should consider the time of year that the trip is to take place. The Ravenglass & Eskdale Railway operates virtually throughout the year, but the service is understandably restricted in the winter. To thoroughly enjoy a relaxing day in Eskdale and Hardknott, catch the first train of the day to Boot and make sure you allow more time than you think necessary for getting back to Dalegarth on your return. It is a long walk back if you miss the last train! There is no reason why the walker should not walk all the way to Hardknott, but it is a long day, so consider catching the train back.

The Ravenglass & Eskdale Railway has a fascinating history; do take the opportunity to enjoy a trip, perhaps travelling in an open coach. The chance to be hauled by a steam engine is rare in the UK and the views are simply spectacular. The railway has a full-time staff aided by volunteers; please support their efforts by considering membership of the Ravenglass & Eskdale Preservation Society:

Hon Membership Secretary
Mr P. Taylor
12 Wholehouse Road,
Seascale, Cumbria CA20 1QY

AN EXCURSION:
WALKING TO HARDKNOTT

This is a long day and to gain the full benefits, a start just after seven in the morning is a must. The walking conditions are variable, but overall good. Be aware of unfenced drops and open water. Supervision of children is required throughout this walk.

Using the Cumbria Coastal Way from Ravenglass beach, follow the old coast road south to just short of the Esk viaduct, where the path passes under the railway, along the river drive of Muncaster Castle, across the A595, through the golf course (keep to the path and watch out for the golf balls). Go along the track at the base of Muncaster Fell and onto Forge Bridge. Keeping to the south bank of the river, the path takes you to Stanley Ghyll and on to Penny Hill Farm. From here the path takes you via the old mine, which seems to have changed the watercourse as the walker then crosses a dry waterfall; out onto the open fell and on to Jubilee Bridge over Hardknott Gill. The way is instantly 'up' and the air is often perfumed by burning brake pads and clutches. This present road zigzags up the gradient; the Roman road, which can be discerned, goes straight up. Keep erosion to a minimum – grass has enough to cope with in these conditions, so stick to the road at this stage, but beware of the cars!

The steep gradient soon ends and, whilst not level, it does ease off for a while. At this point a signpost points the walker off the road to the left. The walker will be glad to be away from the road, as the pass can be very busy, often with clusters of vehicles struggling in one direction or the other, with the inevitable problems of meeting those going in the other direction. The walker can at least consider the strain of climbing the gradient as being easier than the mental torture of trying to drive it! Off the road on the way to the fort the going can be very wet under foot, which is appropriate as the Bath House is the first remain that comes into view. The fort is simply in the most commanding position, dominating Eskdale and effectively blocking the way over the pass.

The condition of the fort, with walls half their original height in some cases, is the result of restoration in the 1950s. The local quarry at Beckfoot had recently closed and the Ministry of Works took advantage of the skilled workforce to put the fort back up. The talented workers merely looked at the piles of stone and just rebuilt the fort as if it were a jigsaw puzzle; they knew exactly how to put it back up again. The Ministry of Works stopped them from completing the job because the academics had little or no idea of how the top should look, having only a few references surviving as to the architecture of Roman battlements. Had the academics just left the men to their work we (the archaeologists) would now know exactly what it looked like, as there is no doubt the quarrymen would have recognised all the key features to put it back precisely as it was. There are piles of stone lying close to the fort; to us they are just stone, but to the quarrymen they were as easy to read as a book.

There are excellent interpretation panels, but forget the detail for a moment – just look at the view and imagine.

Return the same way until you reach Doctor's Bridge (so called because it was extended to allow the doctor's horse and trap to cross) where the walker, if time allows, should cross the bridge, turn right onto the road and spend a while at the Woolpack Inn. If in a hurry, the left-hand turn at the road should be taken – this is a fast albeit less pleasant way to the railway station.

For those not in a hurry, and having been duly refreshed, a short westerly journey on the road towards Boot and a sharp right towards Christ Cliff will provide some entertaining walking on the route to Boot. There are few places where a walker walks on top of a wall, but this is one of them. The path is well marked and the end of this traverse (after a traditional wall squeeze) brings the walker out at a waterfall next to Boot Mill, just over the packhorse bridge on the Corpse Road. Do pay the mill a visit, as the miller is a font of information – ask him about the Corpse Road – and don't forget to support his considerable efforts at keeping this wonderful place alive.

After a visit to the mill there is time for further refreshment at The Boot Inn, formerly The Burnmoor, then spend a while in the Fold End Gallery where there is the opportunity to purchase some extremely fine pieces of local artwork.

The conclusion for the walker is the Brook House at the crossroads, where the station can be seen a short distance away. Here, there is a wide range of real ales of the finest quality – a joy of a place, with friendly family owned comfort.

Simply a superb day out.

WALKING FROM DALEGARTH FOR BOOT STATION

First train up, last train back. Good walking conditions throughout, but just mind the time, as it is very easy to lose a good few hours in the blink of an eye. Again, be aware of unfenced drops and open water, and supervise children throughout the walk.

Out of the station, turn left. Beware – the road is single track and often sees a lot of traffic. At the crossroads by the Brook House Inn – note for your return – turn right to St Catherine's. Spend a few moments at the church and enjoy the river and the stepping stones; you may cross here, but the stones are often underwater and of course slippery, so expect a ducking. Keeping to the Brook House side, follow the path along the river, through the kissing gate and turn right. The path will take you to the girder bridge.

The walker is treading on the abandoned old railway line, which continued from the present Dalegarth terminus directly to the mines. The bridge gives a spectacular view down into the sparkling depths.

Cross over the bridge and follow the wet path alongside the river until a wall line is met. There is a rough zigzag path to get the walker up the rise and the walker should turn left at the top, through the gate and onto the path which takes you through to Penny Hill Farm. This is now the same route as those walking from Ravenglass. Likewise the return is via the Doctor's Bridge.

Day One

Steaming out of Ravenglass

RAVENGLASS TO SEASCALE

DAY 1

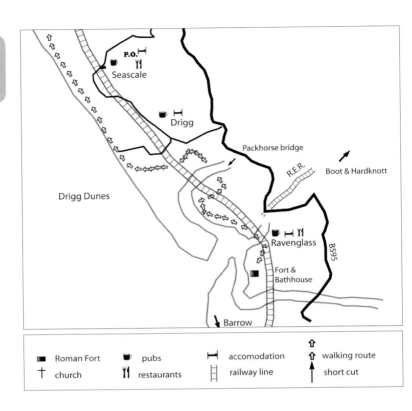

This is a 'get into the swing' day; there is no point pushing things too hard at the start. It is more important to get into the swing than to push the walker's personal limits. If the walker is well-prepared and limbered up, St Bees is possible in a day, but why rush? There is much to see along the way.

The route involves a tidal stretch, tarmac road, soft paths and beach walking. **Difficulty:** Easy going, very little to stretch the limbs, although the beach can be a trudge (the hard sand is easier than the shingle).

The walker can explore Ravenglass at their leisure, but the journey really commences when the walker crosses the Mite viaduct (be aware that at certain times of the year, although you may be able to cross the viaduct, the path to Saltcoats may well be under water – check the tide table and take local advice. Walking the main road to avoid this crossing is not advised.)

The path is good; the Irt wanders in its muddy course to your left, the dunes acting as a sound barrier from the sea. You are constantly reminded of its presence by the seaweed attached three-quarters of the way up the fenceposts, which vainly try to enclose marginal land between the beach and the railway lines to the right. Saltcoats is soon reached, a settlement associated with salt panning and smuggling. There are archaeological sites under investigation in and around Drigg, which will assist in our understanding of the frontier; deep ditches and possible remains of palisades (which in their time were filled depths) await a closer examination. They may well be the first evidence of a physical frontier south of Workington. But that is for tomorrow. The walker, having turned to have one last look back at Ravenglass and the mirror-like effect that a full estuary provides, should then head on the minor road towards Carleton and enjoy the magnificent views to the east. This walk along a broad droving road in open coastal landscape can be a joy in spring, with the dunes just visible to the left and the Cumbrian coast railway to the right. Carleton is a hamlet with a name suggesting a settlement of outsiders or slaves, no doubt given the most marginal of land to survive on in the early medieval period. A small cluster of farm buildings and houses and the remains of two enclosures, probably for holding stock, are seen before venturing through the ford on the way to Egremont. At Carleton the walker should turn eastward, and although there is a footpath to the Irt, it is not advisable to try and ford the river. Head east under a rather fine railway bridge, along the road and then bear left following the footpath (which can be a tad wet underfoot) for Holme Bridge, a medieval structure with associated pastures of great natural scientific interest, so please keep to the track.

There are over 150 species of plant on either side of you, including the red fescue, common bent, crested dog's tail, great burnet, yellow rattle, bird's foot trefoil and lady's mantle, which all thrive in this quiet place, with only the distant sound of the road and the deep, gently flowing River Irt as company.

The River Mite at Ravenglass.

DAY 1

Drigg station and the Queen Vic. Both are worth a second glance.

This path can be very muddy but good, hard standing is soon met as the path climbs up towards Drigg Church. Turn left onto the road, but be careful as the path and road are very narrow at this junction. Take a short walk along the B5344 through the linear settlement of Drigg and then turn left to the well-manicured Drigg station, where a gift or two can be found, as well as a pint to quench your thirst at the Victoria Hotel next door. Take time to explore and rest, for very soon you will walk into a different environment.

Some walkers may consider staying to the B5344, following the cycle route. With increasing amounts of road traffic along this country lane this is not advisable.

The preferred walk is along the road to Drigg dunes, over the railway line, which has the Low Level Radioactive Waste Facility alongside it. The contrast with the high barbed-wire fence could not be greater, and the River Irt swings left as the swathes of tufted dunes draw you towards the sound of the sea. You will pass the northern end of the path from the River Irt and the small Roman fort protecting an earlier crossing, which is under active archaeological investigation. The Roman military way crosses the ford and disappears into the nuclear facility; it should reappear at the northern end of the site, but the railway sidings used during the Second World War, when the site was an ammunition factory, have obliterated any trace. Fortunately, with the indication of a small fortlet in the area and a continuation of the ditch first noted at Saltcoats, the aberrations of the present can be quickly put behind the walker as the dunes beckon.

Drigg sands are a jewel and even in typical Cumbrian weather (horizontal rain at 40mph) the walking is good to Seascale. Along this stretch, the acidic grasslands and heaths support ling, dyer's greenweed, bell heather, field gentian and adder's tongue. It should be no surprise that this is a site of special scientific interest, so keep to the paths and listen out for the toads.

If the tide is in, then take the shoreline path and a short stretch of the B5344 into Seascale. Be careful of the road; at certain times of the day the traffic can be heavy, considering the narrowness of the railway bridge and its rural location.

The walk along the beach is a diversion from the frontier, which we go on because it has a grand view and it's better to soak up salt air rather than

Along the road to Drigg beach.

The final approach to Drigg beach.

DAY 1

Looking back from the cinder track towards 'The Nebb', Seascale.

the car fumes, and also because the frontier route from Drigg to Sellafield is unclear. There are indications of a well-built Roman road crossing the main Seascale to Gosforth road and indications of at least one watchtower site and a milecastle/fortlet, but for the time being, until further work can be undertaken to prove the sites exist, the walker can enjoy the fresh car-free space.

When you reach Seascale there is an opportunity to stock up on refreshments. It is a welcoming spot; a grand little seaside resort that had even grander pretensions that fell by the way, to be replaced with the need for good housing for the nuclear establishment at Sellafield. There are bus stops and a railway station close to the beach. Seascale has a medical centre, pharmacy and post office.

EXCURSIONS

Bus services from Seascale to Gosforth, the 'Gateway to Wasdale', are few and far between, but with the aid of a good map the walker can find a reasonable alternative to the main road, which is an unpleasant bit of walking. Gosforth Church has the finest of all early medieval English crosses, known as the 'Viking' cross. The hall next to the church can trace its foundations back to the tenth century as a result of recent archaeological research.

A trip to Wasdale is possible by means of the Wasdale Taxi Bus Service. This service is operated at bus rates by Gosforth Taxis (01946 725308 on Thursday, Saturday and Sunday). You must pre-book.

As ever, check the Traveline by web or telephone.

Right: *Drigg beach approach; the sea over the hill.*

Below: *A rest in the dunes, Drigg.*

Bottom: *Striding along to Seascale, Drigg beach.*

DAY 1

Left: *Boats at Ravenglass.*

Below: *The remains of Ravenglass Roman Fort, west of the railway line.*

Above: *Not the most crowded beach.*

Left: *Ravenglass Bath House, a remarkable tribute to Roman civil engineering.*

FACILITIES: RAVENGLASS TO SEASCALE

Ravenglass

Restaurants, pubs, hotels, B&B

Ratty Arms: Situated in the Furness railway station. A good family pub with a wide-ranging menu and excellent real ale. One of the finest hostelries in Cumbria.

Pennington Hotel: Recently rebuilt with rooms of international standard, this is a friendly, grand hotel with very fine dining and real ales. Highly recommended by the author.

Holly House: B&B with wonderful views to be enjoyed with a pint.

Rosegarth: B&B. A lovely spot for afternoon tea.

Muncaster Guest House (Muncaster): B&B.

Walls Caravan Park (CCGB).

Jacksons Caravan Park (Saltcoats).

Other attractions

Ravenglass & Eskdale Railway.

Muncaster Castle.

Calder House Hotel, Seascale.

Other facilities
Post office.
'Old Butcher's Shop' gift shop.

Drigg

Restaurants, pubs, hotels, B&B
Victoria Hotel: A restored rural Victorian pub with good food.

Other facilities
Spindle Craft Gift Shop & Café.

Seascale

Restaurants, pubs, hotels, B&B
Calder House Hotel: A period building with fine views, good rooms and
    real ale.
Cumbrian Lodge: B&B with refined dining.
Wansfell: B&B and pub.
Eskdale House: B&B.

Other facilities
Natwest Bank (No ATM).
Health Centre.
Library.
Limited bus service and railway station.

Day Two

Along the Cinder Track

SEASCALE TO ST BEES

DAY 2

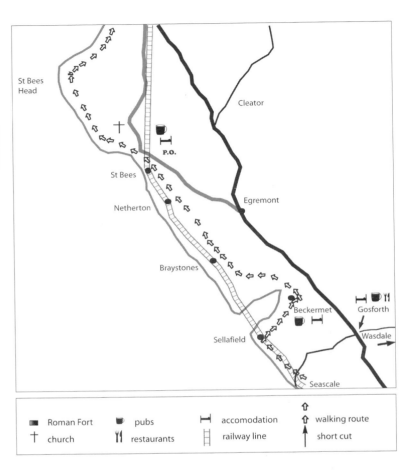

	Roman Fort		pubs		accomodation		walking route
†	church		restaurants		railway line		short cut

A day of marked contrasts – coastal wind-swept dunes, industrialisation on a gigantic scale, glorious solitude, undulating coastal ways and an historic destination at which to rest the limbs. The route from Sellafield is most probably a military way, being the supply route for foodstuffs, troops, tinder and logs, with a good hard surface all the way. **Difficulty:** Very easy going. Beware of traffic beyond Beckermet.

Once refreshed by the sound of the sea lapping on the shore and a good night's sleep, the walker has a choice – either walk along the beach towards Sellafield, or along the 'cinder track' now restored as part of Hadrian's Cycle Route (Route 72). Whichever is chosen the horizon will begin to take on an industrial look.

Why cinder? Because Seascale once had a gasworks, part of a grand design that waned, flickered and went out, the only remains being the cinder from the boilers that came in very useful for the lineside track to Sellafield. The path and the railway approach Sellafield nuclear site directly, side by side, and the walker will possibly hear the occasional cry of 'Fore' as Seascale golf course lies just beyond the railway line to the west.

The landscape approaching Sellafield has changed dramatically over recent years; even parts of the golf course have given way to the boundary of the nuclear site. Only maps pre-1939 provide any indication as to how the river estuary looked and this causes some considerable difficulty for the archaeologist. Rivers, or more importantly estuary mouths, are very difficult to protect, and controlling a frontier is complicated considerably by wide stretches of open water.

There is a good indication of a large, square, raised mound (but not on public land) slightly to the south of the nuclear site and close to the original course of the River Calder, and at a point where the geology forces the river into a narrow. This suggests the possibility of a bridge, all trace of which has now vanished under the later works.

Unfortunately the walker will have to keep to the seaside track, and the River Calder is crossed with the high fence protecting the nuclear works from the walker's accidental trespass. The estuary of the Calder once had a harbour facility, as noted in Elizabeth I's register of ports; it was noted as being abandoned. There is no sign of a harbour and the river has been canalised through the plant. Sellafield has been the source of much controversy over the years on an international scale, but locally it has provided generations with employment. Calder Hall nuclear power station, within the confines of the fence, is the subject of a preservation order. Calder heralded the coming of the 'nuclear age' and was the first commercial domestic-use nuclear facility, a prototype for the Magnox stations that the UK has relied on ever since. Whilst Sellafield appears a daunting site, visitors are welcome. Call at

Above left: *The rimming stone. See what it does! St Bees.*

Above right: *Blooming marvellous. St Bees.*

DAY 2

Above: *From the Manor Hotel the land drops quite dramatically away. St Bees.*

Left: *A quiet moment. Mind the road!*

the main gate and transport will be organised to take you to the Sellafield Visitor Centre – it is worth a visit.

The path is squeezed between railway lines to Sellafield station; turn right, climb the hill and pass the main gate (use the available footpath and mind how you cross to High Sellafield). Follow the footpath to the turn to High Sellafield and then onto the old Egremont railway line, now a cycle path. This route gives you a very fine view of the Ehen Estuary.

The land is agricultural in nature and not public, so please keep to the paths. The closest the walker will pass the site at Beacon Hill is via High Sellafield. These are fort sites, currently undergoing preliminary research, along with a medieval enclosure of Iron Age round houses, making the stretch of headland a very busy spot. All is quiet now and this is pleasant walking, and Sellafield is soon left behind. In the past, before the coming of the coastal railway line, the Ehen was capable of taking reasonably sized trading vessels. It would be unfair to suggest that the railway was the sole cause of the decline in the river – longshore coastal drift, the removal of forestry, better agriculture and mining will have contributed to its navigational demise, a series of factors that will be seen time and again along this walk when rivers meet the sea. But the walker can view the open flood plain and the cows enjoying the pasture and consider the scene a place of peace and beauty. The good path is bordered by purple loosestrife, marsh cinquefoil and bloody crane's bill, providing the walker with fine company and stark contrast to the industrialisation behind them.

In less than half a mile, the walker will have see a major problem for the Romans – the wide river estuary of the Ehen. The predicted headland fort seems so placed as to provide a seascape, as it is set back slightly to allow some protection from the worst of the weather, and the round houses likewise do not brave the crest of Beacon Hill. The second predicted fort site lies further to the east, close by the old railway track which the walker is traversing. It appears to have been involved with management of the estuary, and there are indications of a vicus associated with this site. The frontier cannot avoid this major interruption and manages the area as a large promontory. The military way, with the fort mound noted south of the nuclear site, can as it heads towards Beckermet be considered the main route, with the forts in the area of Beacon Hill on a military-managed spur.

The priory poking out of the trees.

DAY 2

Above
and right:
Blooming.

The path diverts from the old railway line. Take the right-hand turn where the path meets the minor road, and you are close to the church of St Bridget's, Beckermet. Sitting on an ancient raised mound within an enclosure alongside a now dried-up creek, this rather sad little church actually has a wonderful past, and the fact that it has not suffered the fate of many such early places of worship is testament to it being hidden away from view. It is believed that there was a monastery on the site of St Bridget's dating from the seventh century. The site was most likely in use long before the Romans, so the early monastic foundation should be taken in a much wider context. Coastal trading can be traced back over 4,000 years, and this safe little harbour must have witnessed much activity in that time.

Walk under the rather grand little railway viaduct into Beckermet, which offers an opportunity for refreshment at the White Mare or Royal Oak, before leaving again on the minor road to Braystones (be aware – these minor roads see heavy, fast traffic both morning and evening with shift workers heading for Sellafield). The road that you are marching along is most likely the Roman military way which, heading directly north, will keep the walker company, where still practicable, all the way from Ravenglass to Bowness-on-Solway. This service road provides communications and provisions immediately behind the formal frontier.

There are indications of possible watchtower enclosures and bases along this particular undulating stretch of road, and it is most likely that this undulation led to the construction of these apparent watertowers, because of the need to plug gaps in defence and visibility. The frontline, if ever there was a physical one at this elevated location, seems to have gone over the edge, partially as the result of time and partially due to the building of the railway.

St Bees station. Where to next?

The priory still dominating the skyline.

None of these sites have been investigated yet and as the walker traverses this length to St Bees you will note the regularity of the mounds and their precise positioning.

Give us archaeologists time – we will investigate them soon enough!

Note also how relatively protected from the sea this section of the route is, as it makes its way through Nethertown, past Coulderton and onto St Bees. Below, to the left of the walker, is the Cumbrian coast railway line wandering along the beach on a narrow embankment, onto which the sea enjoys the occasional foray when the weather turns a tad inclement, as it is wont to do. This coastal strip is a frontier in itself; the bungalows that stand on the seaward side of the railway act as protection for the line against the sea, and in return for this selfless act the wayside halts for both communities, which remain open for business.

Keep to the road but be wary of the traffic throughout this section to St Bees.

The approach to St Bees provides the walker with a graphic indication of the size of the blockage that clogged St Bees' ancient harbour. The golf course sits astride a very large sand dune with the Pow Beck passing awkwardly beneath its bulk, with suitable reverence for its beached neighbour. Yet the Beck's former strength is indicated by the fact that there is a property called Sea Mill House, and the mill, which sat to the seaward side of the railway, required open water and relied not only on the sea but on a strong inland source to keep the channel open, so the Pow Beck once had a vital role to play.

The walker is soon aware that St Bees is a linear village of two parts – the orderly, smart historic houses are on the south bank, suggesting a deep-seated prosperity with some hidden gems, so do stray and have a look, as it is well worth the effort. There are plenty of opportunities for refreshments as you explore. The station is open; the building, however, is now a restaurant and B&B. 'Platform 9' is a feature of the Cumbrian coast, preserving in its old buildings much of the character of the steam age. At St Bees the wooden station sign remains in place on the building, in contrast to the aluminium examples surrounding it.

DAY 2

A quiet moment, St Bees.

As the walker descends the hill towards the railway level crossing the most striking feature is the wide expanse of openness; the Pow Beck may be merely a stream, but the remains of the harbour are quite obvious to the eye. The priory and St Bees public school dominate the north bank, and the continuity with historic structures stops with them both. Modern St Bees attempts to hide behind the priory with little success and spills down towards the beach. The magnificent priory church of St Mary and St Bega on the northern side of St Bees dates back to the early twelfth century, and is reached by a rather modest bridge over the Beck.

The present priory is perched close to a long-lost waterfront; it was founded by the Benedictines. There are indications of an earlier religious establishment with the remains of Scandinavian-designed cross-shafts burial markers. However, the first indication of a priory is from 1120, when William de Meschin, Lord of Egremont, founded a small priory which obviously prospered as the structure gained in size and worth until the inevitable fall in 1538 under Henry VIII. However, by good fortune the building survived, damaged but repairable, and services resumed in 1611 with the priory now a parish church – it has remained in use ever since.

Erosion at the priory. Your contribution to the priory would help to prevent this.

Good luck perhaps, but it is an indication that there seems to have been very little call on the good stone of the building.

This is at odds with what the walker has come across (or not in this case) ever since the departure from Ravenglass. Apart from the Bath House at Ravenglass, not one vestige of Roman fort or stone-on-stone has been seen.

That is because there are none! That is not to say the forts were built of wood, although some undoubtedly were to start with, but the normal way of things meant that stone was the preferred material. So where did the stone go? The clue is the location: the seaside. The coast is a highway and a trading zone; to this day, ships travel in ballast on the way to pick up goods from one place to transport to another. A captain faced with shingle or nicely cut stone will always go for the stone, because it has value, whereas the shingle does not. Sadly, it does not take a great deal of effort, especially when there is a cash return, to demolish a building.

So Rome left by sea, the same way it arrived.

How the majority of the priory survived is down to the ingenuity of the locals and perhaps the fact that the harbour was by then landlocked, and St Bees stone was relatively easy to acquire directly from the coast – the desire to haul it away as ballast was less. But this is, of course, a theory, and therefore a subject to discuss at the end of good day's walking over a pint or two!

The walker should head for the beach, clearly signposted, and note those fellow walkers beginning, or ending, their coast-to-coast walk by dipping their boots in the sea. The red mass of St Bees Head dominates the view, so enjoy the beach before the climb; there are facilities and St Bees is Whitehaven's beach, so the place is often busy with locals taking the air or enjoying the lovely beach.

FACILITIES: SEASCALE TO ST BEES

Beckermet

The White Mare is a family friendly inn with dining facility.
The Royal Oak Hotel is a small, comfortable inn.
Both are in the centre of the village.

Facilities
Post office, near the Royal Oak.

Above left: *The road crossing the railway, St Bees.*

Above right: *The Manor Hotel in full bloom. A fine pint and good company, St Bees.*

St Bees

Restaurants, pubs, hotels, B&B

Platform 9: Eat and stay at the railway station, an enjoyable spot for fine dining.

The Manor House: A two-bar pub with B&B. Fine ales and a warm welcome in a lively pub at the centre of village life.

Oddfellow Arms: A village pub.

Fleatham House.

Tomlin Guest House.

Stonehouse Farm.

Fairladies Barn.

All are of excellent standard.

Other attractions

St Bees Priory.

Other facilities

Post Office and shop.

Hartley's Café at the beach.

Limited bus service and railway station.

Day Three

Flying High to Whitehaven

ST BEES TO WHITEHAVEN

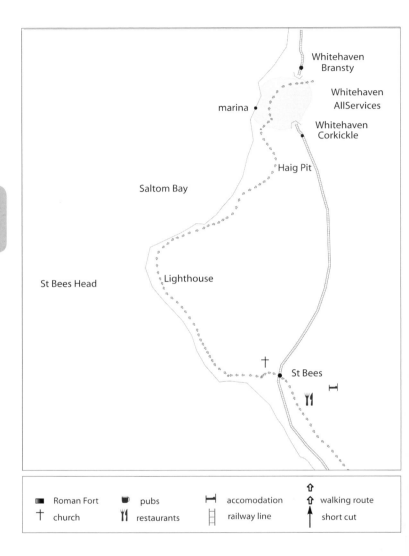

DAY 3

						⇧	
■	Roman Fort	🍺	pubs	⊢	accomodation	⇧	walking route
†	church	🍴	restaurants	🪜	railway line	↑	short cut

This is simply a magnificent and memorable section, and rightly so, as the views are stunning. However, on a less than perfect day it can be a very hard slog indeed. Up on the cliffs the full majesty of the coast can be experienced. This will be a walk of contrasts, from a sleepy old village to remnants of industrialisation to a Georgian port.

Be careful, as there are eroded paths and sheer drops in places. It is slippery in places, with narrows. Take care and watch where you step. **Difficulty:** Fenced sheer drops. Many walkers consider this a reasonably easy path with care, but it can be difficult in some weather conditions. The way improves towards Whitehaven, with hard paths and tarmac on the final approach.

Once refreshed, the walker should head up the heavily eroded path and steps to St Bees Head. This route is heavily used, so take time and care; the route is not for unsupervised children. After the first half-mile the conditions improve, but the erosion of the coast is a constant feature all the way to Whitehaven. Walkers should not attempt to stray from the track. It should also be noted that even the best of walkers miscalculate the distance to Whitehaven because of the dip down and back up to Fleswick Bay, so consider carefully if your pace is slow and the evening is drawing in.

The RSPB identifies St Bees Head as the largest seabird colony in the North West. Guillemots, fulmars, razorbills, kittiwakes and peregrines soar along the cliffs and many vantage points are maintained along this section for the walker to enjoy the view, but don't look down unless you have a head for heights as there is a 100-metre drop! There are always some serious twitchers on this section, no matter what the weather, and if you are not familiar with the birds they will always be of help.

Take your time along this stretch – there is much to take in, as the wildlife and views are truly wonderful, but on a wild day it can be a hazardous place to be. The path to Whitehaven is clear, if a tad narrow

DAY 3

The lockgates that make the marina possible.

The candlestick. Have you found out why it is there? Whitehaven.

and very steep in places. There are traces of the Roman military way, especially just above Fleswick Bay, but the facilities it served have gone over the edge of the cliff.

St Bees Head is the remains of a great desert sand dune and is of significant geological importance. To the north the remains of swampy marshes that subsided into an inland sea provided the wealth of the area: coal. The inland sea left other useful materials, such as limestone and shale.

But that tends to dwindle in the memory (especially any reference to sand dunes) when the wind and rain are giving their best. The location is one of the reasons for St Bees lighthouse, which not only provides a guiding light to those at sea but also meteorological data. The lighthouse has a fascinating history – the first light was erected in 1718 to protect the increasingly busy harbour of Whitehaven and as a guide to Workington and Maryport. The original tower was topped with a coal grate, the idea being that a burning beacon would offer constant illumination, but unfortunately and rather obviously, such a fire was inadequate, and the smoke it generated blanketed the light. The other major problems were cinders, and that the chance of fire was high. In 1822 the inevitable happened, and the tower was utterly destroyed. Joseph Nelson's replacement structure stands as a testament to a good practical design with the use of an oil supply rather than coal. The light is now automatic and electrically powered and is controlled from Harwich.

As the walker begins the descent towards to the mostly hidden port of Whitehaven, you will note some remains close to the sea below the path. These are the remnants of the most important pit in the UK – the

Right: *Once a triangular railway junction, Whitehaven.*

Below: *Tourist Information Centre, Market Hall, Market Place, Whitehaven.*

DAY 3

Above: *Drigg beach.*

Left: *The water tower, Seascale.*

Opposite: *Hidden gems at Ravenglass. Take time to have a proper look.*

A forest of masts in Whitehaven.

site of Saltom Pit dug in 1729, the first coal mine under the sea, possible because of the use of a Newcomen steam engine. The mine shaft was the work of engineer Carlisle Spedding, and was constructed to an unusual but very practical oval shape design, allowing timber balks to be slotted down the centre of the shaft to divide it into 'up' and 'down' sections for ventilation. Spedding showed considerable ingenuity by piping the ever-present and explosive fire damp gas to the surface where it was used to illuminate the mine complex. The mine closed in 1847 and it is hoped that more can be done to preserve the remains for future generations.

The walker will now find that the approach to Whitehaven is a gentle downhill one in scenery contrasting to that of late. The remains of Whitehaven's chemical industry at Marchon are slowly being wiped away, and the once-busy yards of the pits on the clifftops are now no more than grassy open spaces. The path is good, being the course of a long-abandoned railway line passing the Haig Pit, with its pit winding gear standing gaunt against the skyline. King Coal has all but been wiped from the map, but Haig acts as a testimony to the community's past, and it is well worth a diversion to the museum.

Facing north, the remains of an incline taking coal to the harbour can be seen, but keep to the well-made path to get you down the final slope. On the way some further major remains become apparent – the monumental candlestick chimney and the castellated walls and grand lodge of Wellington pit, and then the strangely evocative Guibal fan house which used to provide a fresh air supply to the Duke pit, stand like true Roman remains, like the arch of a long-lost bath house. The scene is quiet now, but all the activity of mining, the hauling of wagons, loading of ships, steam whistles and the activity of the harbour with ships arriving and departing for far-off lands must have made Whitehaven a dramatic soundscape, something no restoration or rejuvenation can ever quite capture.

The Beacon Centre is your first port of call to get your bearings, as there is much to see and do. The author allows you a free hand and foot as long as the walker finds the way to the Bransty railway station (Whitehaven has two stations, the other being Corkickle at the St Bees end of the town), and then finding the way to Moresby is assured.

The coastline here has been quarried and mined for centuries, so there is little opportunity for the Romanist in Whitehaven, but plenty for the industrial archaeologist. The cliffs around Whitehaven are crumbling, areas

DAY 3

The start of the C2C cylce route.

Above: *Fortifications on Drigg beach.*

Right: Acme, *Ravenglass. Ravenglass would not be a port without her.*

Opposite above: *Holly House Hotel, Ravenglass. Great views at any time, but especially sunset.*

Opposite below: *Ravenglass Bath House. Still standing and with internal decoration still in place.*

Lowther Street, Whitehaven.

are dangerous and fenced off, including areas of the beach. The way into Whitehaven is well marked and you are introduced to its maritime past in a revitalised rather than preserved environment.

Whitehaven is a grand Georgian port (historically important in the rum trade), with a history best explored at the Rum Centre on Lowther Street. A major part of the reason for the impressive layout of the town was that Sir Christopher Lowther wanted to keep an eye on his ships arriving and departing for Africa and America from his home, Whitehaven Castle. The grid of streets grew around this principal thoroughfare.

Whitehaven Castle is a Grade ll listed building, constructed in the seventeenth century as a residence, and the term 'Castle' was added later. It was originally known as the 'The Flatt', remodelled in the eighteenth century under successive Lowthers, and was given to the town by them for use as a hospital. It was a scene of dereliction until the 1990s when it was restored and converted to apartments. It is an outstanding credit to the town.

These grand streets contain many fine examples of captains' houses, testament to the port's expansion from nothing but a beach to a port to rival Bristol in less than 100 years. There are plenty of places to ease the feet, quench dry throats and dine on excellent fish and chips, straight from the fishing fleet that still calls at the port, now mostly used as a marina.

The keen landscape observer will have noticed that Whitehaven lies in a deep valley bottom and that it is merely a couple of miles on the map around to St Bees, although for obvious reasons only the railway takes the

The pier master's house, Old Quay, Whitehaven.

DAY 2: SEASCALE TO ST BEES

Above: *St Bees Head viewed from a Northern Rail train.*

Opposite above: *The priory church of St Mary and St Bega.*

Opposite below: *St Bega, St Bees.*

The marina. A splendid regeneration of a run-down harbour, Whitehaven.

easiest way round, avoiding the bulk of St Bees Head. The keen contour-watcher will also note that the southern road route from Whitehaven to St Bees keeps well out of the valley bottom until St Bees proper, and likewise the footpath from the northern approach keeps a respectful distance up the slope until it reaches the priory, suggesting how damp the valley can become. The walk over from St Bees has been effectively on an island. As Whitehaven grew in importance the harbour facilities moved out towards the sea as every bit of space closest to the water's edge was taken up; thus, some properties have cellars that were part of earlier harbour walls. Nature, as it will, often causes the valley bottom to flood with inevitable consequences for parts of Whitehaven. St Bees, having long fallen into disuse as a harbour, takes care to keep its feet out of any potential flood. The walker can enjoy the harbour and the sites; it is hard to believe that less than twenty years ago it was a run-down port with dereliction on all sides.

The direction for the walker is ever northwards, and the route takes the traveller towards Bransty railway station.

FACILITIES: ST BEES TO WHITEHAVEN

Whitehaven

Restaurants, pubs, hotels, B&B
Whitehaven has a great number of places to find good dishes, and there are some excellent B&Bs and hotels. This is a small selection:

Arrighi's Chip Shop: Historic fish and chip establishment.
Espresso Café: Situated in the market place, this is a popular spot with cyclist and walkers. Excellent breakfast menu.
Glenfield House: A home from home atmosphere in grand Victorian style, just up the way from Whitehaven castle.
The Waverley Hotel: Set in the centre of town, this fine Georgian town house offers excellent value accommodation.
Glenfield House.
Chase Hotel.
The Rum Story (Café & Museum).
Akash Tandoori.
Ali Taj.
Blue.

Above: *The great priory door, St Bees.*

Opposite above: *Looking across to the priory over what was once a waterscape.*

Opposite below: *St Bega, St Bees.*

DAY 3

A hearty meal is required now and again! One of the finest.

Casa Romana.
Crosby Seafood Restaurant.
Cross Coffee Shop.

Moresby

Moresby Hall Country Guest House and Cottages: A wonderful historic house with magnificent period rooms. Highly recommended by the author, so book early and stay a while!

Other attractions
The Rum Story (Café & Museum): Absolutely smashing!
The Beacon Centre.
Haig Pit Museum.

Other facilities
Railway station has a booking office.

Day Four
Along the Old Track
WHITEHAVEN TO WORKINGTON

Above left: *St Nicholas' Church. A fire in 1971 devastated the building except for the clock tower and entrance.*

Above right: *The market place, Whitehaven.*

A view of the busy marina at Whitehaven.

Scudding clouds, Whitehaven.

Around the market place, Whitehaven.

DAY 4

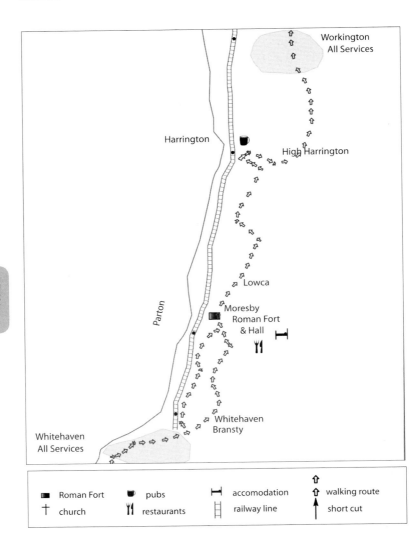

This is a stretch connecting two very different powerhouses, Whitehaven and Workington, comprising wonderful coastal views, industrial archaeology and some old railway lines finding new uses, all making for a good mix of views and experiences.

The route keeps to footpaths at a slightly raised contour away from the modern coastline. At High Harrington, after a visit down to the harbour, the way is simple to follow and brings the walker into the heart of Workington. The walker cannot be anything but amazed by the contrast in situation; the new shopping centre is set to kick-start a new era in the town. **Difficulty:** Good surfaces throughout. There is a climb up to Moresby, if the walker has not stopped at Moresby overnight and again at Lowca, but otherwise it is very easy going. Some traffic to cope with.

Once refreshed, the walker should head past the approach road to the railway station, and proceed to walk up the hill and immediately turn left onto Bransty Brow, at which point the walker has a choice of route.

Turn left again for the low-level walk.

The William Pit Disaster Memorial: on 15 August 1947, 104 miners, many just back from fighting in the Second World War, died in an explosion at William Pit. Whilst Whitehaven had suffered many disasters before, this single event had an enormous effect upon the town. The memorial stands at the pit head, yet there are few obvious remains of the once-busy colliery, but the memorial is a testimony to the town's attachment to this tragic event.

As one walks up Bransty Brow, the walker will be aware that the walk to Moresby Roman fort is a steep one, but the effort is worth it and not quite as daunting as it may seem (if you take the footpath signposted roughly halfway up the brow on the left). This is roughly the route of the military way and this becomes clearer the further north along the path towards Parton. The upper route has clear indications of the remains of the Roman military way heading for Moresby fort; this will mean a stretch along the main road (A595) before turning left towards a very purposeful-looking church and an equally splendid house bedded in against the ravages of the wind to its right.

The lower route goes via the remains of William Pit and onto an old railway line beneath the cliffs that make up the brow; do not stray too close as the cliffs occasionally drop the odd rock to remind the passer-by of their presence. The walk takes a higher contour than the present railway and the walker has a good view back towards Whitehaven, and the way is easy into the village and ancient port of Parton. The relaxed approach has to be paid for and there is a steep hill, Brewery Brow, which balances out the easier going for most of the way, which takes the walker up for a very brief bit of A595 walking. The A595 is not a pleasant experience, but there is a good footpath and the walker will be aware of the left turn toward the imposing edifices of the church and hall.

Moresby's Roman fort, Gabrosentum, known from the inscription found at the site to have been a cavalry base, stands overlooking the Solway, a level platform at the top of the cliffs, with the railway line snaking around the base, lapped by the sea that once provided a safe beaching point for shipping. This is an imposing spot and the fort's site was undoubtedly meant to be one, preventing any invading force from considering this relatively easy beaching point. The fact the fort was a cavalry establishment suggests a rapid reaction force patrolling the coast.

DAY 4

Opposite above and below: *Jane Pit, Workington – a magnificent survival of a castellated engine house. Well worth the effort to seek out; a rare piece of industrial history.*

Artwork at Harrington. A major regeneration of this derelict harbour is under way.

DAY 4

Jane Pit,
Workington.
A forgotten
industrial gem.

The fort site is partially occupied by the parish church of St Bridget's, and Moresby Hall stands on part of the vicus, the civilian settlement. This very grand property, with works by Inigo Jones and later William Thackery, is well worth a second look, if not at least a night's stay, as the hall is now a guest house of considerable atmosphere and stately charm.

The present road past the church is roughly the fort ditch; when repairs to the wall and road were undertaken some years ago, a vast number of bones were excavated, suggesting that the fort ditch had been used as a charnel ground upon the new church being constructed. One way of getting a good road surface!

Having surveyed the fort site the walker must consider the hill up to Lowca, past the water treatment plant built on the site of the famous Fletcher Jennings Lowca Engineering works. This is where many steam locomotives were built, exported all over the globe and in some cases are still going proud, notably Talyllyn No.1, built in 1864 and still pulling passenger trains on the railway of the same name.

Whilst the beach looks a safe option to walk to Workington, it doesn't give the views. Instead, the walker should head upwards, though there is no official access to the cliffs. In this instance, as the cliffs have a tendency to slip down into the sea, it is perhaps heartening that there is not. Hard to comprehend that there was once a massive works perched on them. Lowca clings to the sheltered side of the hill and is a mining village, and the site of Harrington No.10 pit, closed in 1968, is on the walker's left.

The road can be a busy one; much has been done to slow the traffic, but caution should be taken as the village is left behind, and the walker will need to look for the Cumbria Coastal Way sign, pointing west, that will take them towards Andrews Gill.

The scenery is very different from that of the cliff section from Braystones to St Bees; there are echoes of an industrial past all the way to Harrington. However, there is also an indication of watchtower enclosures, yet to be investigated, suggesting that the old Lowca Light Railway line (built to move coal from Harrington No.10 pit) is taking advantage of an earlier track.

There are stunning views but the walker is always conscious of a slight air of abandonment; at the same time the half-heard sound of wagon wheels is made only too real by the passing of a real train on the coastal line below

The small port of Harrington, built in 1760 by Henry Curwen, comes into view. The path drops you down to enjoy a few moments at the harbour which is worthwhile, before climbing back up the hill, along the footpath towards Grayson Green. From there turn left along the road and then right across the stream, and up the lane to the A597. Turn right and then cross the road. Be careful crossing the road, and turn left into the remains of High Harrington station, now no more than bushes.

DAY 4

Site of the Lowca Engineering Works.

Opposite top: *The approach to Senhouse Museum. The Battery, Maryport.*

Opposite middle: *The new bridge over the inner dock by the lock gates.*

Opposite bottom: *A Cumbrian coastal moment, Maryport.*

Right: *A beacon of hope. Maryport is reviving its good fortune.*

Below: *Safe moorings, Maryport.*

High Harrington boasts a local shop, just up the hill from the railway footpath, and a farm shop a little further along the same road, which is close to a suspected Roman fort site, yet to be investigated. Interestingly, at the bottom of the hill there is a local belief that a Roman temple lies beneath St Mary's, Harrington's parish church. This belief probably lies in the finding of a chunk of Roman altar, which was incorporated into the structure dating from the twelfth century.

At the station site turn left along another old railway line which takes the walker right to the heart of Workington. The walker will note that this is Route 72, so expect a few cyclists to join you along the way.

The old railway line is met by another coming in from the left, just after High Harrington station is left behind. In the field just beyond, at Salterbeck, a large Iron Age double-ditched enclosure was found by means of aerial photographic research. This site is located at the top of the valley which leads down towards the present Harrington harbour and appears to be a cattle keep. This is similar to an enclosure above Ravenglass, indicating that cattle movement by sea was regular and profitable long before the Romans.

Walkers will wonder why the route leaves the coast at this point. The answer is that whilst there is a coastal path, the coast has changed dramatically over

Harrington harbour. The first signs of regeneration, now under way.

DAY 4

the centuries; the recently closed steelworks, specialising in rail-making, has lately dominated the seaward side of the town and from a Roman perspective, this vast area would have either have been beach, or shallow estuary waters. Using the abandoned railway line to gain access to the heart of Workington is a compromise. The railway keeps to a reasonable contour and was very roughly the first bit of land mass above the shoreline in Roman times. Following the exact contour is simply not practical.

Iron-making is in the very blood of Workington, the reason being the location. There is a plentiful supply of water, a coastline for shipping the product from, and coal and lime all on the doorstep. The method employed for the most part was the Bessemer process, using haematite pig iron for the production of steel rails, but there were also brass foundries and ball-bearing works, rivet manufacturers and railway spike production. Corus were the last operator of the site, the last part of the iconic blast furnace complex having been demolished in the 1980s. There was a plethora of independent companies producing metal on various sites. One name, The Lowther Haematite & Steel Works, highlights the integrated nature of commerce in West Cumbria, in this case the connection that the coal-owning Lowthers at Whitehaven had with the production of steel.

This is a well-maintained stretch that should really have a train on it. The closure of Workington central station in favour of the more distant facility towards the harbour has inevitably backfired, as Workington has recently undergone a massive regeneration and the town centre is well worth a visit to restock. At least the walker and cyclist can enjoy the remains of the infrastructure.

Whilst in Workington there are a few short excursions that will provide an insight into Workington's past; start at the seat of the Curwens at Workington Hall. There are great plans for the revival of the Hall to provide a training centre for young people and an exhibition and events venue for the town.

You can see what the hall used to look like at the Helena Thompson Museum, housing a wide collection of pottery, silver, glass, and furniture, revealing the social and industrial history of Workington.

There are two significant, if overlooked, memorials to coal production in Workington, and they stand side-by-side on the appropriately named Annie Pit Lane. They are the preserved remains of the Jane Pit; undoubtedly some of the most ornate pit head structures you will find in the UK, and the remains of a gin circle, where a horse was used to power a winding engine to bring coal up from the depths, and immediately next to it are the remains of the steam-powered replacement, constructed in 1843. The pit was the property of the Curwen family of Workington Hall. With the demolition of the rail production plant these ornate

A holiday villa with a charitable purpose at North Lodge, Allonby.

Between sea and sky, Allonby.

Allonby in bloom.

buildings will soon be all that Workington has to remind the visitor of its industrial past.

If there is one single piece of evidence of the coastal change in Workington, it can be found at St Michael's Church, east of the walker's route. A seventh-century foundation, continuously remodelled ever since, and recently rebuilt after an arson attack, this site stands high on a bluff at the edge of the ancient estuary mouth, now lying land-locked.

AN EXCURSION BY BUS – COCKERMOUTH: 'A GEM OF A TOWN'

DAY 4

There is an excellent and regular bus service from Workington to Cockermouth. Architectural historians please note, Workington bus station is the first purpose-built, covered bus station in the country, opened in 1926. Take a closer look – it really is a very grand building.

The journey to Cockermouth only takes twenty-one minutes and as you approach, the Northern Fells can be seen in the distance. Keeping you company is the Derwent, and not far from the bypass roundabout as you arrive in Cockermouth, up on the hill to the left, is a Roman fort, probably Derventio. (Roman historians will note that Derventio also appears for a fort at Little Chester in Derbyshire.) The settlement of Papcastle sits on top of it and there have been a series of excavations of the site, notably by Time Team in the late 1990s; as usual there is nothing above ground to see.

Above: *Date of works above the door.*

Right: *A Silloth moment.*

Alighting from the bus the walker will soon realise that Cockermouth has been and continues to be a prosperous town, with some notable pieces of mostly Georgian architecture. Principal buildings include the childhood home of William Wordsworth, which is open to the public. Operated by the National Trust, the experience is well worth the time; the author shall say no more, as it would spoil it.

The castle is privately owned and is best viewed from the entrance to Jennings Brewery, which offers a tour of its facilities. Some of the castle's fortifications lean at an alarming angle and the walker can return to the vertical after a visit! There is an interesting debate about the origins of the castle – there is a suggestion that the original Norman wooden structure was destroyed by Robert the Bruce c.1150, and subsequently rebuilt in stone, with much of the current ruin being of fourteenth-century origin. However, there is a reasonable claim that the original Norman wooden fort was at Tute Hill and, after its destruction, the decision to build the fort on a new site was taken. Tute Hill was considered to be a windmill mound, but English Heritage and the author consider it to be the motte of the earlier castle. Archaeological research has not yet taken place to prove it beyond doubt!

The position of the present castle, sitting at the convergence of the Derwent and the Cocker, is a prominent one. Below its walls is a whole warren of trades and services, and the part of Cockermouth on the castle side of the River Cocker is distinctly different than that on the Workington side. Cockermouth still has proper shops, greengrocers, a plethora of butchers, two ironmongers, a proper bookshop and galleries. There are numerous places to eat and drink and the author recommends '1761' in the Market Place. Ask the landlady why it was so named.

FACILITIES: WHITEHAVEN TO WORKINGTON

Workington

Restaurants, pubs, hotels, B&B
Fernleigh House, High Seaton: A Georgian house in quiet setting.
Washington Central Hotel: Centrally based; a touch of quality.
Hall Park Hotel: Good food, good location, comfortable accommodation.
Henry Bessemer: Old cinema, now a Wetherspoons pub with good ale.
  Named after the inventor of the Bessemer process – appropriate for the location, if only as a memorial.

Wide, cobbled streets in Silloth.

Beautiful scenery and wonderful views feature throughout this journey.

A beautiful Silloth sunset.

Other attractions
Helena Thompson Museum.
Workington Hall.
Jane Pit.
Workington Church.

Other facilities
Railway station has a booking office (peak hours).

Cockermouth

Pubs, restaurants & hotels
Allerdale Court Hotel: A wonderful setting in the Market Place.
Six Castlegate Guest House: Historic setting.
The Trout Hotel: Near Wordsworth House.
The Bitter End: Magnificent pub with its own brewed beers.
1761: New pub in a wonderful Georgian building.
The Grey Goat: A friendly locals' pub – give it a go!
Fletcher Christian Tavern: Town pub with live music.
Hunters: Town pub.
The Black Bull.
The Bush.
The Tithe Barn.
The Kingfisher: Simply excellent!
The Swan Inn.

Other attractions
Jennings Brewery tour.
Wordsworth House.

Other facilities
All, save for no railway station.

Day Five
Ancient Coasts & Windmills
WORKINGTON TO MARYPORT

Above: *Holme Cultram Abbey, Abbeytown, which was damaged by arson attack. Please help this church rise again.*

Left: *A welcome sight! Newton Arlosh.*

Above: *A fourteenth-century fortified tower of St John's Church, Newton Arlosh. Please don't forget to make a contribution to its upkeep.*

Right: *Striding out for Bowness-on-Solway. Almost there!*

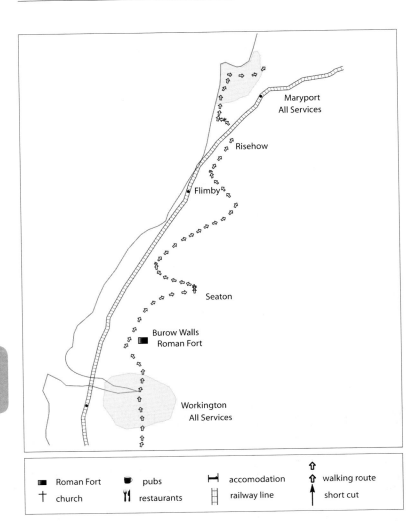

DAY 5

There is no way to describe the scene of a wood-pulping plant and chemical works as being pretty. It is not. However, there are islands of nature, Siddick Pond in particular. The windmills sitting next to the railway line are an asset to the location. The walking is surprisingly good and Maryport is easily reached. After the day from Whitehaven to Workington the walker will have an understanding of the dramatic change in the coast from Roman times. **Difficulty:** Very easy going, some edge-of-field work and a main road to cross, but otherwise good. Some road walking on minor roads.

Staying on the railway line, the walker crosses the Derwent on the remains of the railway embankment, and the new bridge provides excellent river views.

Wherever possible the Roman army avoided getting its feet wet and considerable effort was put into river crossings, and in many instances on this walk the present-day efforts are less impressive than the Romans'. Some estuaries could be marched round without problem, such as the Ehen and Calder, without compromising the coastal frontier structure; however, the Derwent at Workington must have caused considerable difficulty and the site of the Roman crossing is a subject for continuing debate.

The track skirts North Side housing estate and the walker should take the right-hand path as the track diverges. Soon after this junction the remains of Burrow Walls are reached – this is a Roman fort site, possibly Magis. Although the standing remains appear to be a re-use of the Roman fort structure as a bastle – a fortified farmhouse, very prevalent in Cumbria in the days of cross-border raids from Scotland and the activities of the Border Reivers – they at least provide some physical remains to look at. This fort stands a little above the coastline as it was at the time of the Romans. The large wood-pulping plant to the west of the site is built on the remains of an ancient harbour facility; large, vertical cut timbers were found when the foundations were being dug and hurriedly covered up before the archaeologists could get near them. The site of the fort just above such a seaward commercial site is no coincidence.

A splinter of ancient stonework incorporated into the wall at Senhouse Museum. The Battery, Maryport.

DAY 5

Opposite above: *Anthorn.*

Opposite below: *The end in sight: Bowness Banks.*

More outstanding natural beauty for the walker arriving from Wallsend. What wonders lie beyond?

Left: *The great lock gates at Maryport's inner dock.*

Below: *New footbridge, Maryport.*

Bottom: *A reconstruction of a Roman watchtower at Senhouse Museum, Maryport.*

DAY 5

Just to the left of the fort is Siddick Pond and it's well worth a short diversion. In the middle of this partially derelict landscape is a little haven. Many species of birds use the site for breeding and overwintering on, including the little grebe, tufted ducks and little terns, darting in and out of the Canadian pondweed and water horsetail. This area homes a migrant population of black-tailed godwit and marsh harriers finding solace by the waters under the cliff known as Oyster Banks; another piece of evidence of a changed coastline.

Continuing along the old railway to the village of Seaton and then turning left back down the hill, the walker says farewell to the line that has been a constant companion since High Harrington.

A River Clyde steam tug in the inner dock, Maryport. Why not find out more?

DAY 5

The new bridge at Maryport.

Opposite above: *A detail of the mosaic in the small pavilion. The Banks, Bowness-on-Solway.*

Opposite below: *Bowness-on-Solway – the end of the walk from Ravenglass, and the start of the Hadrianic walk to Wallsend.*

A ghostly Solway sun.

Above left: *Maryport's inner dock.*

Above right: *Bew bridge, Maryport.*

The way to the sea, Maryport.

Taking the right-hand footpath at the back of the factories at the bottom of the hill, the walker is walking the old coastline proper and the countryside contrasts with the chemical sites to the west. The ridge does show signs of a constant ditch-like feature, just in from the edge, and the occasional small enclosure – as usual, yet to be fully investigated. The walker is away from the road and traffic and has open pasture to the right; there is occasionally livestock in these fields, so take care.

The Siddick wind farm adds an interesting skyline for a while but the walker can enjoy fine walking and not need to drop down the slope further, by taking the right-hand path after St Helens and then the first left. After climbing further up the slope to keep to the high ground, the path will take the walker past Flimby cemetery, through the upper part of the village, and then take the track towards Penny Gill and New House Farm. Bear left at the junction of paths and then bear left again towards Risehow and the first recorded archaeological site since Burrow Walls. The track down the hill deposits you onto the main coast road. To your left is a spot called Fothergill, which is the site of a Roman watchtower, next to the remains of the Risehow coke ovens. Extreme care is required at crossing this road. Turn right and head towards Maryport.

The modern road cutting at Risehow is the site of a Roman watchtower, or signal station and milefort, depending on your interpretation of 'signal station' and 'watchtower'. The site appears to have had at least a milefort and a separate tower at different periods, along with a small Roman farmstead close by. This is an interesting location: a knoll, cut through by the sea, railway and road, with a Victorian house making the most of the view on the northern end.

It would be no great surprise to the walker that there is nothing readily visible of the site's quite busy past, but the archaeologists can confirm the spot. There is higher ground behind Risehow which the walker has descended to reach, along the footpath, and this whole section of countryside warrants further archaeological investigation, as the cluster of structures at Risehow and the nearby sites at Fothergill, Whitecroft Bridge and Balnakeil Forge suggest an intensive Roman agricultural system right up to the frontier's edge.

If the earnest map-reader takes note of the contours around Maryport they will notice how much of it, to the south, is virtually at sea level. It suggests a larger natural port than the constructed one of today. But enough archaeology for the moment – save that for the future. The walker deserves a breath of sea air.

Just past Risehow the road meets the Cumbria Coastal Way and seaside; Maryport is also just a short walk away – simply cross the railway line by the road bridge and enter the town via the Maryport Solway Park, which provides a seaward side path that leads to the port. This stretch is well worth a visit, as there are clumps of disparate grasses, home to the rare purple yarrow broomrape.

Maryport, once a small coastal port, was greatly developed by the Senhouse family in the eighteenth century and remained viable until the fall of coal. However, our Romanists will want to head for the Senhouse Museum and Roman fort on the northern headland. The uphill route to this is well signposted and takes the visitor through a well-laid-out town with signs of a prosperous past and the first signs of a better future, for a major regeneration project is well underway. Plenty of places to eat and drink exist, and if you pick July to visit there is the world-famous Blues Festival to enjoy.

Left: *More lock gates, Maryport.*

Below: *Maryport – absolutely splendid!*

DAY 5

Alvana Roman fort is the first physical remain since Burrow Walls and there is plenty of information for the walker and Romanist alike. The most significant remains, from a Romanist point of view, are the altars; the dedicatory inscriptions that have proved invaluable in identifying military movements around the empire as well as individual officers and events. This is also the best opportunity to stand on a reconstruction of a watchtower, and it really will give a whole new perspective to how these relatively simple structures dominated the landscape.

Please support the work carried out at the museum, by emptying wallets and pockets at this location. Why not become a Friend of Senhouse Museum? There are some very exciting times ahead, with a new museum planned which will offer further opportunities to study the Western Frontier.

Senhouse Museum
The Battery
Sea Brows
Maryport
Cumbria CA15 6JD

Roman Britain needs you!

DAY 5

Above: *The Battery, Maryport.*

Right: *Senhouse Museum, The Battery.*

Silloth-on-Solway's RNLI lifeboat station. Support them!

FACILITIES: WORKINGTON TO MARYPORT

Flimby

Post office.

Maryport

Restaurants, pubs, hotels, B&B
Riverside B&B.
Harbourside Guest House.
Shore Walk Guest House.
Cross Quays Fish 'n' Chips.
The Lifeboat Inn & Harbour Restaurant.
Waverley Hotel.

Other attractions
The Lake District Coast Aquarium.
Maritime Museum.
Senhouse Roman Museum.

Other facilities
All.

Day Six

Roman Beachcombing

MARYPORT TO ALLONBY

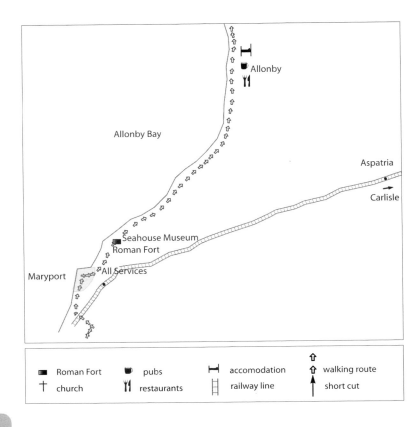

■	Roman Fort	■	pubs	⊢ accomodation	⇧ walking route
†	church	¶	restaurants	▯ railway line	▮ short cut

This is the start of a most wonderful section of the walk – a walk along the cliffs and the prospect of Allonby Bay stretching away into the distance. The beach can be tiring under foot, but it is much better than the road. Stay off the road if you possibly can, for it is a busy one. Allonby is a welcome sight and the walker may be tempted to go further, but the rest is worthwhile. Enjoy. **Difficulty:** In poor weather this can be a hazardous section. Consider wisely before setting out if the weather is rough; tides can be high and furious. On a good day, it is a joy. Hint: a tide table is useful for this section.

Once refreshed, the walker has a choice of how to depart from Maryport: either the Cumbria Coastal Way, closest to the sea, or the Allerdale Ramble. Whichever the walker chooses, the route northwards into the Solway coast is designated as an 'Area of Outstanding Natural Beauty', but that should soon be apparent as the landscape changes from pastured clifftop to open coastal sand dunes and beaches

The author's preferred route is out of the museum, turn right and along the cliff path. However, if you prefer a change from the seaside and want to get a scale of the Maryport site then turn left out of the museum, round the fort site along a high-walled footpath, left at the next junction and then after a short distance the road peters out. Turn right down the hill and then nearly immediately turn left back up it, through Bank Farm, which with your assistance will be converted into a new museum in the near future. Continue along the path contouring its way back to join the Allerdale Ramble route, meeting it near Bank End.

This route, whilst certainly not the quickest, has provided the walker with a sense of the scale of the Roman site at Maryport. Allowing for that which is lost under the later town, there is a vast swathe of hidden structure, suggesting a large population, which has yet to be explored.

The walker is now in the presence of the B5300. The beach is the walker's refuge and is part of the Allerdale Ramble; head towards Brown Gill Roman fortlet, and in doing so you will drop down to cross the gill. There is good evidence that this is the site of a northern port at Maryport, now lost to the sands. As ever, more work is to be done regarding this intriguing site and as always the walker needs to take a closer look.

Looking towards Allonby from Crosscannonby salt pans.

DAY 6

Allonby from near the beach.

For the more earnest map-reader those contours may be of interest; follow the stream back from the coast towards Ellen Grove and then the River Ellen to the harbour, and you will see that the bulk of Maryport is in fact sitting on an island. There are echoes of the Whitehaven and St Bees geography.

From this point on, the walker is in the Solway coast 'Area of Outstanding Natural Beauty'; please respect that fact. The area is of international importance for bird life, rare plants and landscapes, sand dunes, salt marsh, raised mires, sand, mud flats and rich agriculture. The walker will get to visit every aspect in the next few days.

DAY 6

North Lodge, Allonby.

Allonby Old Baths. A grand edifice, now a private residence.

The fishing village heart of Allonby.

Above: *Plenty of green.*

Left: *Between sea and sky. Crosscannonby salt pans.*

If the weather is with the walker this is a magnificent section; if not, it can be extremely exposed and possibly a tad dangerous, especially if walking the road in adverse conditions. So be careful how you go across Allonby Bay.

The frontier from Maryport to Silloth-on-Solway is better understood than most – not that there is a great deal for the walker to see in the way of remains, save for one reconstructed site and that is currently out of bounds. Just stick with it – we archaeologists will prevail and your walk is part of the process. Who knows what you might find as you travel along?

Before you reach Swarthy Hill, milecastle 21 hoves into view on your map, just across from the saltpans and on top of the bank to the walker's right. For once there is a substantial remain for the walker to have a look at, or there would be if access was permitted. Alas, the steps up to the fortlet were decayed and the infrastructure awaits repair, the way blocked until such time as funds allow.

This is a standard Roman milefort, a robust stone-built structure within an enclosure with an outer ditch. There is enough surviving to suggest that the Romans knew enough about the prevailing weather conditions to keep the worst of the weather out. There are two gates with small barrack and administrative quarters either side of the main entrance. The site was thoroughly investigated by Turnbull in 1998 and you can find the details in *Transactions of the Cumberland and Westmoreland Antiquarian & Archaeological Society*, 91 (1998), pp.61-106. Now the walker may be wondering where to see a copy of this work – all good Cumbrian libraries have the 'C&W' and your nearest is Silloth-on-Solway (ring on 01697 332195 for opening times). For those reading this guide in advance of the walk the 'C&W' is an invaluable guide and can be accessed via the web or in your local library if you order the volumes. The C&W actively supports archaeologists working in Cumbria, and you too can support them, so do get in touch via the website: http://www.cwaas.org.uk/

DAY 6

Above left: *Crosscannonby salt pan, Allonby Bay.*

Above right: *A pint of Yates bitter, which is available along the route at many of the pubs listed. Yates is brewed by Yates Brewery in Westnewton, Cumbria, just off the route near Allonby.*

Have a good read and you will see that archaeologists have done something; give us the resources and we will do much more!

Alongside and below the milefort, next to the road, is the well-preserved Elizabethan salt pans. Salt was made from seawater, of which there was no shortage locally. The large circular structure is the sleech pit, sometimes known as a kinch. Cobble-walled with a clay infill, the floor was covered with reeds providing a filter system and salt-laden sand was gathered from the shore in a hap, a horse-drawn rake. The remains are in reasonable condition, but the other features of the process are in constant battle with the weeds and brambles. Do take time to have a look, and whilst you do, consider how much things have changed along this coast. The sea still plays an economic role, but from tourism; the days of extracting a wage directly from the sea have long gone.

From Swarthy Hill, Allonby is soon in view. The formal frontier structures are for the most part invisible, but the walker soon begins to get the impression that the ridge to the east takes on that formal role. This is understandable, because it largely does. It may be no more than a slight rise in a field, but there is a tangible echo. Where roads or footpaths allow divert from the main path and have a look for it.

Allonby is a welcoming site with the opportunity to rest – a historically popular stop, one that Charles Dickens and Wilkie Collins enjoyed, staying at the Ship Inn. There is some wonderfully diverse architecture in Allonby, mostly built for and by Quakers, the principal building being North Lodge (1840) at the north end of the village. This is the work of Thomas Richardson, a major shareholder in the Stockton & Darlington Railway. The central pavilion was his summer home, with the accompanying wings used as homes for widows of the parish. It is still a very grand establishment, now social housing, so continuing in its original role and providing a stately aspect to the coast.

In the square stands a well-proportioned classical portico – the frontage of the Allonby Baths, built in 1835 by a member of the Clarks shoe family. Well-proportioned in architectural terms but strangely out of scale with its environment; as the walker will note, Allonby has a very curious mix of grand properties intermingled with vernacular structures. There is a curious charm about the place that is hard to put one's finger on; there is the seaside atmosphere on the one hand and the genteel stately charm on the other.

Perhaps the most important structure is the Reading Room, which you cannot fail to notice by its striking Victorian design. Built in 1862 for Joseph Pease, it has until recently looked very much the worse for wear, but is now rising from decay with a magnificent level of craftsmanship which is a tribute to the original designer Alfred Waterhouse. Waterhouse cut his teeth on this structure and he went on to design the Natural History Museum in London and the Prudential Insurance Company building in Manchester.

Amazing what you can find on the Cumbrian coast!

Needless to say there is no obvious sign of the frontier except the ridge at the back of the village. But do wander off the main track and enjoy the exploration – there are nooks and crannies to explore.

FACILITIES: MARYPORT TO ALLONBY

Allonby

Restaurants, pubs, hotels, B&B
The Ship Inn: 'A Dickens of a place'. An inn with a grand atmosphere. Good real ale from the nearby Yates Brewery. On a windy night it is a wonderful, warm place to be.
Baywatch Hotel.

Other attractions
North Lodge: Private property.
The Baths: Private property.
The Reading Room: Currently under restoration.
Christ Church.

Other facilities
'Twentymans': village shop and post office.

HADRIAN'S WALL HERITAGE LIMITED

It is official – the wall is a limited company!

> Hadrian's Wall Heritage Limited was set up in 2006 by One NorthEast, the North West Development Agency and other partners. It is a not-for-profit company whose role is to co-ordinate protection, development and promotion of the Hadrian's Wall World Heritage Site. The Wall is already one of the best-known ancient monuments in Europe but it has the potential to generate even more economic and community value.
>
> The company's aim is to realise the economic, social and cultural regeneration potential of the Hadrian's Wall World Heritage Site and the communities and environment through which it passes by sustainable tourism development, management and conservation activities which benefit local communities and the wider region. All this is done in a way that reflects the values embodied in the World Heritage Site Management Plan.
>
> Extract from: http://www.onenortheast.co.uk/page/hwh.cfm

Or, in other words, using good commercial methods to improve the lot of the people who live with the past and the visitors who want to come and look at it.

And jolly good luck to them – it's about time something positive was done to improve the public facilities of what is a magnificent World Heritage Site. The 'other partners' include English Heritage and Natural England, local councils, the county councils and a myriad of others. All committed to making things better.

Importantly, HWH Ltd is actively promoting community involvement and particularly 'Community Archaeology' which benefits all, because if local people better understand their past, that past is more likely to be cared for and we can all enjoy it to the full.

DAY 6

Day Seven
Quick March to Mawbray
ALLONBY TO SILLOTH-ON-SOLWAY

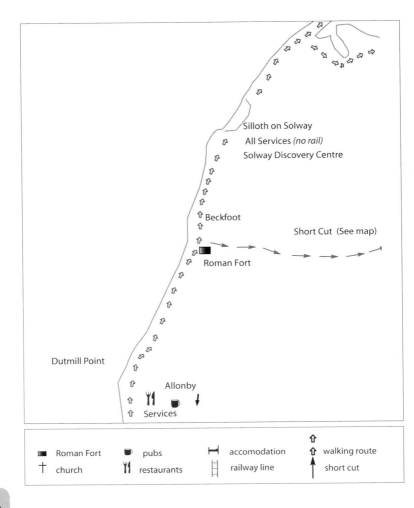

■ Roman Fort	🍺 pubs	⊢ accomodation	⇧ walking route
† church	🍴 restaurants	⊟ railway line	↑ short cut

DAY 7

More beach walking, avoiding that road wherever you can; which is not always possible, so take care on this section. The view behind as you travel north puts Allonby in a wonderful perspective. For those going inland the contrast is very apparent; this is good walking in lovely scenery on lanes and drove roads. **Difficulty**: Easy-going beach walking and hard standing routes. For those taking the 'Roman Shortcut' have the map ready, but the way is well marked. Hint: A tide table is useful for this section.

Once refreshed, the walker should head north along the beach passing Salta Moss. The frontier keeps to the seaward side and the small fort at Dubmill Point is soon reached. There is also a watchtower slightly to the north of the point. If you walk by the road be extremely careful of the traffic as you traverse this section.

March along Mawbray Bank with the opportunity to try and spot the fort in the field to the south of the shore-side car park near Beckfoot Farm. The fort has been excavated and the name is known, so Beckfoot is Bibra. The walker can imagine what a tour of duty would have been like – on a good day, a wonderful posting, but on a bad day, the worst in the empire!

So much has been made of the conditions along the northern-walled frontier (Hadrian's Wall) as a consequence of the discovery of the writing tablets at Vindolanda that the harshness of the western posting has been overlooked. But the Roman cremation sites here at Bibra have provided an amazing depth of evidence as to the consideration the Romans gave to the dead. No basic funeral pyre at Bibra: the dead appear to have left this world in some comfort, on feather mattresses, good beds and to the smell of pine. This level of comfort may well compare badly with that available in life.

The bird population does not seem to mind as this is a favourite nesting spot for whinchats, linnets and stonechats, and their comfortable situation is due to the efforts of AONB volunteers. Through their labours the birds have thrived and you should be able to spy a good few more, depending on the time of the year, including curlew, grey partridge, lapwing, redshank, snipe and yellow wagtail – there are interpretation boards along the coastal strip to help you work out the myriad variety.

Yet this stretch of coast and its hinterland around Mawbray Banks had been a place of residence long before the Romans decided to place a frontier here.

DAY 7

Striding out along the beach, north of Allonby.

A Silloth sentinel.

Back in 1988, archaeologists discovered a settlement on the ridge just east of Mawbray, encircled by a ditch with a semi-circle of posts forming a structure on one side of the enclosure, which was dated to nearly 4000 BC.

A ROMAN SHORTCUT

Walker please note: this shortcut means you will shorten your journey by one night!

For the walker who wants to try a piece of genuine practical research work, try this shortcut to Abbeytown.

Why?

The land beyond Beckfoot Fort hardly makes it more than a couple of metres above sea level in solid form, the western seaward side being sand dunes. The estuarine eastward side is the result of those industrious monks who did their very best to turn marginal land into good grazing and agriculture, making Silloth-on-Solway little more than a marginal hump in a sea-tossed river wetland. The Romans would be more than aware of the problem of trying to have an effective frontier with estuarine mudflats and fast-changing rivers.

The Romans managed to construct a milefort at the Silloth-on-Solway end of Grune Point, effectively providing a view of open water on the west and east side at the time of its construction. This must have been an extremely vulnerable position. This has led the author to consider an alternative or additional frontier, at the very least a formal military communication route to Kirkbride from Beckfoot to supplement this exposed location. The walker is part of the process of discovery, turning theoretical archaeology into fact. Let the author know your findings: hadrianscoastal@googlemail.com

On a grand day this is a truly wonderful walk across some stunning, gentle countryside, so it would not surprise the author if the archaeological research comes a very poor second to leaving the land untouched!

Just north of Beckfoot Farm, take the footpath to Mawbray Hayrigg, then along the track crossing past Wolsty Springs; the footpath diverts from the track to West House, while the original Roman road carries straight on following the contour. However, the diversion is a short one. Turn left on the Coldmire road and take the first right past Prospect House and on to Pelutho.

The walker will notice the route now is on higher ground and, whilst the road wanders a tad, the general direction is straight to Abbeytown. At Pelutho bear left and just past Pelutho House, and as the modern road bears right, take the footpath straight on into the field. The path skirts around the fields here towards Foulsyke Farm. There is much of archaeological interest along this section; which means, as ever, much to do but no funds to do them with!

DAY 7

Busy moment in Silloth.

From Foulsyke Farm turn left and along the road to Highlaws, then left at the end of the Gale, and Abbey Cowper appears in the distance, the name reminding the walker that the lands traversed have all been part of the monastic living of Holme Cultram Abbey. Beware of the traffic when joining the B5302. The walker is now on the approach to Abbeytown, where this shortcut meets up with the other routes to Holme Cultram, Abbeytown. If not taking the shortcut, and if you decide to continue northwards along the bay, do take time to have a look at the Beckfoot Quaker burial ground, in use from the late seventeenth century until 1990.

After Woolsty Bank take a right turn off the beach and then left at the beginning of the fields, and the path will take you along the edge of Silloth-on-Solway golf course and on to West Silloth-on-Solway. Where the good track joins the road, turn left and virtually immediately left again, out onto the dunes – thus avoiding the need to cross the railway bridge – and follow the dunes round to the docks and climb up the hill into the quite remarkable architectural centre of Silloth-on-Solway.

Silloth-on-Solway probably comes from 'sea lathes', grain stores (silos) by the sea, which is quite appropriate as the later port saw much importing of grain. Modern Silloth-on-Solway was constructed as a tourist destination by the Carlisle and Silloth-on-Solway Bay Railway Company in 1856 and has streets set out as cobbled boulevards, built on the grid pattern. It seems quite an appropriate settlement for this walk to pass through. It is

DAY 7

a substantial but different sort of place, set down from another culture on the Cumbrian coast, reminiscent of Roman forts and vicus which in turn would be at odds with the native environment. It is a delight, if a tad decayed, and the loss of the railway seems to be the heart of this malaise, for Silloth-on-Solway was Carlisle's seaside, but it is most certainly worthy of survival and the residents should be congratulated on their efforts. There is no shortage of places to stock up on supplies and all the basic infrastructure and facilities you would expect from such a community.

The Solway Discovery Centre is worth a visit and will assist in the walker's planning of the next stage of the trip, for there is yet another change of scenery ahead. The centre offers an informative look at the history, environment and development of the Solway coast and, most importantly, it looks forward rather than just back. Mind out for Auld Michael the Monk and his companion Oyk the Oystercatcher! The building also acts as an administrative headquarters for the management of the Solway coast.

More importantly, just outside under the grass is a milefort, No.11 in the modern sequence.

Right: *Golf Hotel, Silloth.*

Below: *Half-expecting a hansom cab to go by, Silloth.*

DAY 7

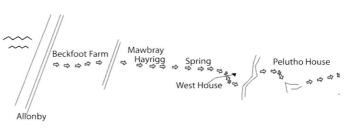

Silloth on Solway

Beckfoot Farm
Mawbray
Hayrigg
Spring
West House
Pelutho House

Allonby

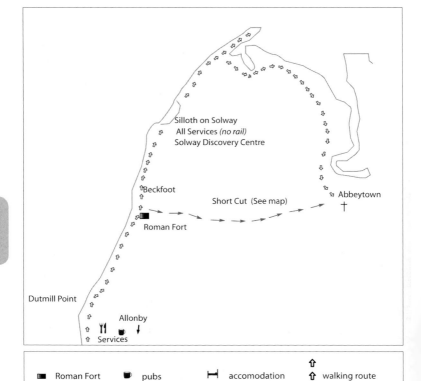

Silloth on Solway
All Services *(no rail)*
Solway Discovery Centre

Beckfoot

Short Cut (See map)

Abbeytown

Roman Fort

Dutmill Point

Allonby

Services

■ Roman Fort	☕ pubs	⊢⊣ accomodation	⇧ walking route
† church	🍴 restaurants	railway line	↑ short cut

DAY 7

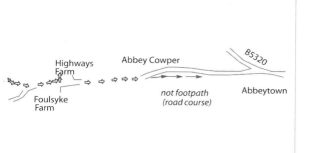

Above: *Shortcut.*

Opposite below: *Day 7 route.*

Right: *River Waver at Rumbling Bridge.*

Below: *Dubmill Point.*

DAY 7

FACILITIES: ALLONBY TO SILLOTH-ON-SOLWAY

Be sure to stock up on necessities here, as the opportunities further north are extremely limited!

Restaurants, pubs, hotels, B&B

Golf Hotel: In the heart of Silloth-on-Solway, popular with golfers and visitors alike. Friendly atmosphere.

West View Guest House: A lovely, fresh and bright guest house. Excellent value.

Criffel Inn.

Cumberland Inn.

Silloth Café.

Blue Dolphin Café.

John's Plaice.

Other attractions

Solway Discovery Centre: An absolute must and a good place to check the next part of your route.

Other facilities

Banks.

Buses.

Library.

Health Centre.

GETTING INVOLVED IN ARCHAEOLOGY

DAY 7

Whether the walker decided to take the shortcut to Abbeytown or not, his desire to explore is at the very heart of the activity – otherwise walking is merely a matter of going from A to B. Walking is having the opportunity to look close up or stare in amazement at an ever-changing landscape. The landscape is constantly changing not just because of walking through it, but because it will have changed the moment it has been walked through by the walker, imperceptibly perhaps, but it will have changed. Millions upon millions of tiny actions erode or construct the scene, with mankind constantly attempting to make an indelible mark. Wanting to know what yesterday was like is at the heart of archaeology.

Having spent over twenty years studying the Romans on the West Cumbrian coast the author is perhaps now able to change a full stop to a comma on the amount we know, perhaps adding a sentence or two. That gives you a sense of the scale of the task.

The walk to date has taken the walker through several centuries and different phases of the Roman occupation of West Cumbria, a complex series of events, some quite probably being played out long before formal Roman military control reached into the territory of the Carvetii, the sub-Brigante tribe occupying parts of Cumbria.

Current research suggests Roman-affiliated coastal trading was being carried out as a precursor to the campaigns by Petilius Cerealis in AD 71, followed by Agricola's likely estuary-based west coast temporary camps and forts in AD 77-8, with Trajanic forts providing a fluid defence, renewed and strengthened by Hadrian in AD 122 onwards.

And that is just for one small bit of the local landscape in Cumbria and only accounts for the early years of Roman influence; there are at least another 300 years to go!

That of course is just the Roman part; there are thousands of years of mankind to look at, to study and to get involved in, wherever the walker hails from. This walk offers a Roman bias, but the industrial heritage of West Cumbria might inspire the walker just as much.

The glorious thing about archaeology is the fact that it is not all digging holes; there are a myriad of ways in which anybody can get involved. So how do you get involved where you live? For starters join the CBA. Every part of Britain has some story to tell which is woven into our soils, landscapes and buildings. This historic environment is one of our richest resources and gives a special quality to our lives. It is also irreplaceable. Yet, because we live and work in it, it is easily overlooked or squandered. Nothing stays the same. Changes made the past, just as they will shape the future. We owe it to those who follow us to find ways of managing change so that they will have a past for themselves. This is why the CBA exists: to give a voice to Britain's past, and to help enrich the time to come. The CBA is a network of individuals and national and regional organisations which cover Britain. It welcomes everyone with a concern for our historic environment. By joining us you:

Give us resources to develop our work in education, conservation and providing information.

Strengthen the profile of archaeology in the minds of decision-makers.

DAY 7

Individual membership also brings:

Six issues of our flagship magazine *British Archaeology*, including CBA Briefing with projects and events in which you can be involved.

Three issues of the Members' Newsletter, with news of the latest CBA projects and initiatives.

Membership of a CBA Region.

A voice in the work of the Council.

Our Annual Report.

Find out more at: http://www.britarch.ac.uk/

To join the CBA as an individual member, send £32.00 by cheque/postal order/money order in sterling to the address given below (or use our secure online shop at http://www.britarch.ac.uk/shop/index.html to pay by credit card). Joint membership is available for two individuals living at the same address for £38.00. Student membership is £19.00 (proof of accreditation required). Membership of our Young Archaeologists' Club costs only £12.00. Combined family membership, including membership of the CBA and YAC, is also available for £40.00.

Council for British Archaeology
St Mary's House
66 Bootham
York YO30 7BZ

Telephone: (+44) (0) 1904 671417
Fax: (+44) (0) 1904 671384
Email: info@britarch.ac.uk

Day Eight

Mud, Monks & Marshes

SILLOTH-ON-SOLWAY TO ABBEYTOWN

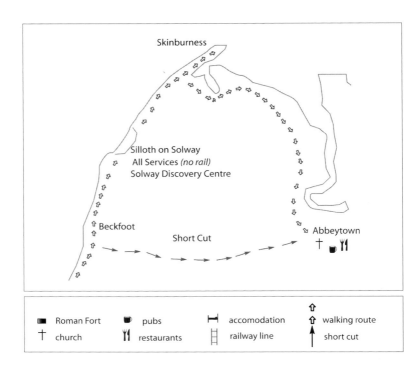

The way out to Grune Point is an enjoyable stroll on a good day, but a windswept experience when not. Yet it is worth the effort for the views. The marsh makes for some difficult conditions and the walker is reminded to keep to the recognised route. If weather conditions are poor stick to the road, which is, I am afraid, a relatively busy one. Good views 'viewed with care' is the best approach for all these circumstances and conditions. Conditions for walking do improve closer to Abbeytown, but the walker will have to mind the road throughout. **Difficulty:** Beach and marsh, variable but good if weather is in the walker's favour. Hard standing on roads.

Once refreshed, the walker should use the Discovery Centre as a point from which to restart the journey, mostly because the walker can re-check his plans, and the author stresses the need to be well aware that the next section really does require a good map and common sense as to where (and if) to tread. If weather conditions look unfavourable take the safe option every time.

From the Solway Discovery Centre head westward and turn right towards the Cote Lighthouse; the cobbled road has come to an end, and the formality of Silloth-on-Solway falls away, as the elements begin to take over. The walker will note a turning to the right to East Cote Farm; under the farm lies milecastle No.10.

DAY 8

The walk to Grune Point is a cheerful one, but as ever the smile may be wiped away in bad weather. Do take a look at the pillbox – it is part of our history and of a design unique to Cumbria. Likewise, the birdwatching opportunities are considerable and the whole of the bay is a haven for twitchers. The archaeology of this section is uncertain – from personal research and that of others, where the frontier lies is uncertain. It probably skirted Morecambe Bay rather than be allowed a break. The Rivers Wampool and Weaver stagger towards the sea through mud and sand; do not wander onto them with the intention of trying to cross the bay. For the purpose of this walk the passage will be across the reclaimed lands, but may change in future editions of this guide, as evidence of our Roman past comes to hand.

Above: *Whitrigg Bridge over the Wampool.*

Right: *The Wampool.*

DAY 8

Above left: *Holme Cultram, Abbeytown.*

Above right: *Holme Cultram showing some of the damage. The entire roof of the Abbey has been lost.*

From Grune Point the path takes you around and back to Skinburness, where the decision has to be made as to which route to take. The Great Gutter acts as good warning, so it is up to the walker to make the decision – use common sense and follow the proper way and you will have an enjoyable journey to Rumbling Bridge. This is a spectacular section for anyone with the slightest interest in wildlife. Forget the Romans for a while, and enjoy nature in the raw.

Those deciding not to cross the Great Gutter can make their way along the ancient sea dyke. The road is good walking, if busy, and provides clear evidence of the desire to enclose the land, for agriculture goes back into the mists of time. At Hartlaw stay on the road and then bear right to Calvo. Turn left to Waitefield, as this takes you off quite a busy road, especially in summer. Whilst there may be a temptation to go over to the bay there is no public right of way beyond Seavill Cottage, so turn left for Beech House. At Beech House turn left through Seaville, and at the road junction the footpath continues straight ahead. Head towards Winding Banks to avoid the road and rejoin the trackway. Turn right to Rumbling Bridge and turn right again. Both road and path are heading for Abbeytown passing Samden House which stands on the first bit of high ground in some time; this area is worthy of archaeological investigation in the near future.

DAY 8

Top: *A place of warmth and comfort. Newton Arlosh.*

Above: *Scudding clouds on the Solway: The embankment of the old Solway viaduct is mid-distance.*

Right: *Newton Arlosh Church – built to withstand the ravages of man and sea.*

Skinburness – a windy day!

Abbeytown is dominated by the church of Holme Cultram Abbey, now in restoration after a recent arson attack. Fortunately the Cistercians' great construction of 1150 was more than a match for the arsonist; whilst the roof was destroyed, the walls withstood the conflagration and stand as proud as ever. Please support the appeal by making a donation at the Abbey shop.

Across from the Abbey is a rather forlorn-looking building, of some great age and not without distinctive signs of a more profitable past. This is the Old Wheatsheaf Inn, the birthplace of Sir Walter Scott in 1826, a self-made man whose civil engineering ability focused on the construction of underground railways. His talent founded a vast fortune and business empire, yet he never forgot his home village and restored the Abbey. That work has to be done again now.

FACILITIES: SILLOTH-ON-SOLWAY TO ABBEYTOWN

Abbeytown

Restaurants, pubs, hotels, B&B
Wheyrigg Hall Farmhouse Hotel: A comfortable hotel with a fine menu of local dishes.
Wheatsheaf Inn: A village pub with good food and shop.

Other attractions
Holme Cultram Abbey (currently undergoing repair).

Other facilities
Post Office.
Bus service.

DAY 8

Day Nine:

A Walk on the Wild Side

ABBEYTOWN TO BOWNESS-ON-SOLWAY

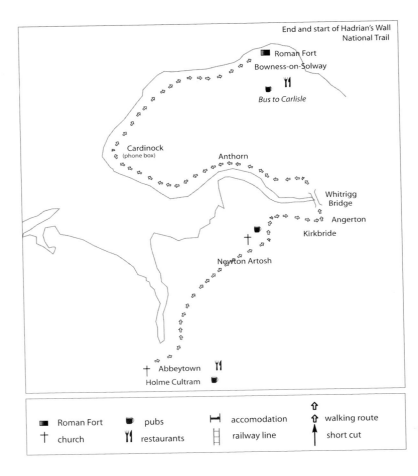

The walk to Bowness-on-Solway involves some pleasant road walking; the way is not a busy one, for the most part the hedges are set back, save for some severe blind bends, and the features of ancient droves are apparent with countless herds being moved to and from the rich estuarial flats. The flatness of the route is far from boring and the views at dusk can be amazing. Plenty of natural history to keep you company. **Difficulty:** In bad weather and high tides the way across the Wampool can be blocked. Take reasonable care with the bridge as there is no path. Hint: Check tide for Whitrigg Bridge.

Walkers will note that the author has included details of mileforts on this section from Cardunnock onwards, primarily to give a countdown to Bowness-on-Solway, and secondly because the sequence, at least of mileforts, seems reasonably secure from Cardunnock to Bowness-on-Solway. This cannot be said for the area south of Cardunnock, as the renewal and repositioning of watchtowers there means that we find duplications within a very small area. Not forgetting the fact that we have not necessarily found them all yet, which means the numbering system needs constant renewal!

Once refreshed, the walker leaves via the road to Raby. At the staggered crossroads take the left turn and then left (straight on) at Grange Bridge. The walker is again down on the marshlands; it soon becomes obvious that the landscape is familiar as the road takes the walker back on himself, a somewhat dispiriting feeling in bad weather, as the route heads towards the aptly named Salt Coats, a witness to the industry of this land.

The going is flat through Maryholme, West End and Middle Farm and into Newton Arlosh. Newton Arlosh is a comfortable, prosperous settlement. The church is of particular note, being one of the finest fortified tower churches of its type, built in 1303 when the village was set up to replace the inundation of Skinburness. Perhaps of equal note to the weary traveller is the Joiners Arms a short distance away. Beware of the road by the pub. Throughout this section of the walk the hedgerows are a constant joy and the number of verges are more than adequate for the walker. However, as these lands were set down to agriculture in a managed fashion, the bends tend to be sharp and blind.

After a few minutes rest at the Joiners Arms, take the right hand turn off the B5307, and just after the abandoned railway line crosses the road take a sharp left back across it and along the Monks Dyke. This will take you to Kirkbride, site of a Roman fort. Pottery found at the site was initially dated to the second century; however, a much earlier date of AD 80 is now attributed and it is belived that this site is Portus Trucculensis, mentioned by Tacitus in the *Agricola*, making Kirkbride part of the Stanegate system of forts.

Time will tell and no doubt there will be a good deal of dirt under the fingernails before it is proven! In the meantime try the Bush Inn, Kirkbride, for a much-needed rest (check opening times in advance). This linear village leads onto the turning for Angerton – take this turning and a short distance ahead is Whitrigg Bridge, where the walker can at last cross the River Wampool, the last major barrier before Bowness-on-Solway. The bridge is narrow without a proper footway. This section of the walk can be blocked by high tides. Always take local advice and do not try and cross if the road is submerged.

This section of the walk from the Wampool to Bowness-on-Solway can, in inclement weather, be an unpleasant, windswept experience; make sure you have the appropriate waterproofs ready to hand. At the T-junction the walker should turn left for Anthorn and Carrdunnock. The sign will suggest turning right for Bowness-on-Solway; a mere three and a bit miles away. But if you do you will miss some of the finest views yet, so left it is. The way is easy going, little traffic passes this way and the road beyond Cardunnock is used more by cattle than cars. The roads are gated along the estuary section and the views are truly magnificent.

Anthorn is a mixed community, with housing bearing the strikingly Ministry of Supply style of 'HM Forces domestic', resulting from the days of the airfield, in contrast to the traditional Cumbrian farms and Victorian residences, set in a magnificent alignment along the Wampool estuary. The agricultural nature of the settlement still remains, with the farms clustered along the roadside. There is evidence of a potential fort site at Anthorn, discovered by aerial survey.

Anthorn's increase in scale is directly the result of Cardunnock Airfield. Sleepy though it may appear now, since the closure of RNAS Anthorn (HMS Nuthatch) in 1958, Cardunnock is a very important place in time; the time signal is broadcast from here. Listen for the hourly pips!

According to some Roman military historians there should be a Roman fort at Cardunnock, or more precisely round about the site of the airfield, but either the enormous and now abandoned airfield destroyed it, or more likely we simply have not found the exact location yet. The airfield has some interesting military structures still standing; these are just as important in archaeological terms as our Roman past. Old radio huts are the equivalent of beacon stations and watchtowers.

For my part I think the Roman frontier line is further back than the airfield (which appears to be sitting on a more recent beach) and that milefort No.5 is the turning point of the frontier line as it follows the contour of the land. My reasoning is that the village of Cardunnock sits on a little island, about 10 metres above sea level. The contour watcher will note that there is one area slightly higher at 15 metres to the north-east and then the 10-metre contour turns south, skirting around the airfield. The author's suspicion is that the line of the frontier lies beneath this 10-metre contour edge, heading down towards Mary's Tower and the potential fort site at Anthorn. You never know – this might be the site of the missing fort at Cardunnock!

The long walk around the airfield is good underfoot, but the remains of the military establishment, now mostly barns or cattle shelters with a series of herding pens on one of the runways, is an odd, ghostly spot.

The gorse rustles at a distance and deadens the sound of the sea, which is closer than you think, yet in this wild expanse there is a feeling of being watched. The huge straining wires of the masts make you aware that you are in the presence of silent giants. Just before you leave the complex of wires and masts behind, hidden beneath the sod lies milefort No.5 on the left.

The very small hamlet of Cardunnock, much more attractive than the airfield that has usurped its name, is reached, with a telephone box its only public amenity. This is most definitely very rural Cumbria. In Roman times there was a watchtower here, over to the left of the village, and extensive defensive ditches and here, quite possibly, the walker has just stepped

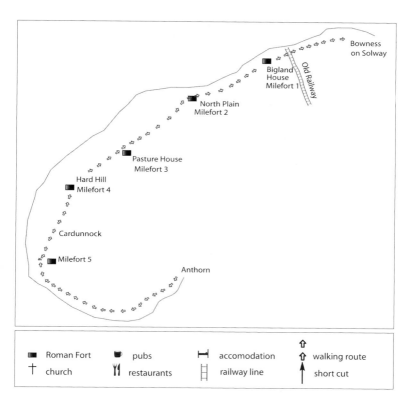

back onto dry land, having crossed, if my theory about the direction of the frontier is correct, what was a beach.

The single-file road staggers out of Cardunnock with a view of the Scottish side of Solway in the distance; this will now be a constant companion to Bowness-on-Solway. On the opposite bank is the busy little town of Annan, in contrast to the gentle solitude the walker is treading.

There is a definite change in the climate as you turn into the Solway proper; as soon as Cardunnock is left behind and the Scottish coast has hoved into view the scenery changes. This is a factor that was not lost on the Romans, as just before the track turns the walker passes milefort No.4 on the left and the site of a series of cremation burials.

Tall beech trees line the track and, whilst the force of nature cannot be ignored, the fact that trees can survive is testament to the local micro-climate. All the way past Herd Hill and Pasture House, the site of milefort No.3, the land is perceptibly improving.

Cattle enjoy the freedom of the estuary; these inquisitive creatures should be treated with respect and care. Never attempt to run away from a cow, although it may be tempting if a good few are intent on saying 'hello' at a rate of knots. Remember a cow has four legs, you have two. If you feel worried, simply raise your hands in the air, wave them about and make a loud noise. The result is amazing – the cows will stop, look puzzled and back away. Continue the arm flapping and yelling until the way is clear. Repeat as necessary for they will be back. You can't keep a good cow down!

The signs alongside the road declare that this area is Campfield Marsh Nature Reserve, which covers both sides of the road and extends into the hinterland and its peat bogs, with a wide variety of bog plants and attendant

Above left: *Scotland across the way.*

Above right: *Cardunnock. Rural or what!*

Left: *Neat and tidy farm buildings in the centre of Bowness-on-Solway.*

Below left : *The farmhouse in detail. A clear indication of re-used stonework, possibly from the Roman fort.*

Below right: *Bowness-on-Solway churchyard with indications of earlier structures beneath.*

Above: *It seems further on foot! You are standing in the Roman fort here.*

Right: *Floral moments on the Edwardian Promenade, the banks of Bowness-on-Solway.*

summer dragonflies. Well worth a detour, but keep to the marked trails. After Maryland Farm and the site of turret No.2, look out for the right turn to North Plain and the RSPB hide, which is a short walk down the track.

North Plain is the site of milefort No.2. This is also home to the Cumbria Wildlife Trust site, so look out for the badger symbol. Both organisations deserve your support and they have done much to improve the lot of the natural habitat. Right next to the road is Biglands Farm and the walker may be able to spy some irregularities in the field here, as this is Hadrian's Wall milefort No.1.

Milefort No.1 had three periods of use, but it seems to have been derelict by the mid- to late second century. It was fitted out with a small barracks, two cookhouse facilities and had one entrance overlooking the Solway. The fact it had relatively excessive cooking facilities strikes the author as odd, as it was so close to Bowness-on-Solway, suggesting that when a tour of duty on the frontier commenced, luxuries such as popping home when off duty were forbidden.

All of a sudden the walker is faced with a bit of an up, which is curious considering the locality. This is the bridge over the Solway Junction railway – to the right is Bowness-on-Solway railway station, now a private property, the line having long since closed. The walker may have been curious as to the stone embankment sticking out into the Solway on the approach to the bridge. This is the remains of the Solway viaduct, a none-too-profitable edifice, but the result of a good idea to connect Cumbrian haematite with Lanarkshire coal directly, rather than by the overcrowded railway system at Carlisle. A slight problem of land ownership on the Scottish side and the enormous cost of the viaduct, plus the Bowness Moss to cross, meant the line started off on

DAY 9

the wrong foot and stayed that way. The line saw considerable traffic in the First World War but the viaduct, having suffered natural disasters and the odd collision, was closed to traffic in 1921 and eventually demolished in 1934.

Famous more for the Scottish Sunday drinkers heading south into England in the era of Sunday observance than for anything else, apart from the odd casualty going over the edge, the remains of the Solway viaduct serve as a lesson in how humankind believes things permanent, when huge efforts and works can just disappear in the twinkling of an eye, leaving only cursory traces. No doubt if the author had not pointed out that the hill was in fact a bridge, the walker would have wandered on none the wiser. That is how much the physicality of the present means to the future – it is a thing most likely overlooked.

From this point Bowness-on-Solway is in sight; a couple of pretty cottages and the rather uninspiring but very practical bus turning circle greet you. Perhaps not a grand finale, but there again it is the first sign of public transport in a long time and it is better than nothing! Having observed the lack of a 'Welcome to Bowness-on-Solway, You Have Made It' sign the walker should proceed up the hill, past the school on the right and into the village.

Bowness-on-Solway is the Roman fort Maia, and is technically the start of the Northern Frontier, Hadrian's Wall, and so it is the terminus of the Western Frontier. I might add that the 'technical' bit has been added by historians over the centuries and more recently by heritage management. We have no absolute evidence that the end or beginning is at Maia, and most likely over the centuries of Roman control the emphasis on the practicality of border patrols would have varied, but for our purposes it will do as a stopping point.

DAY 9

How many days has it been since Ravenglass?

There are similarities with Ravenglass – both are coastal communities, but Ravenglass has a purpose-built facility for long-distance and coastal vessels. Perhaps there is one at Bowness-on-Solway – we will see!

Maia means 'larger', a big fort, equal to anything else built along the frontier. The early fort was of wood and turf bank construction, the latter of stone. The author considers that there may in fact be an earlier phase than the presently known one, with a fort on a different axis to the latter two. Controversial stuff, which will keep fellow archaeologists busy over a pint or two on a cold winter's night!

Bowness-on-Solway has seen archaeological excavations; in 1967 the Durham Excavation Committee organised a dig, and for those studying before travelling the report is available from the archives of:

Archaeological News Bulletin, Northumberland, Cumberland, Westmoreland
    12/1971/17
The Journal of Roman Studies 59/1969/205
University of Durham Gazette 15/1968/2:17

In 1955 the then-Ministry of Works had a go by the North Gate:

Transactions of the Cumberland and Westmoreland Antiquarian &
Archaeological Society 60/1960/13-19
POTTER,T.W./1979/ROMANS IN N.W.ENGLAND/321

You see, you are doing research already!

For those walkers not doing their homework, the fort at Bowness-on-Solway mostly lies immediately under the village, and there appear to be signs of a vicus under the church and the field in front of it; situated possibly as a result of prevailing weather conditions, with the fort taking the brunt of the winter gales. It is possible this vicus is taking advantage of part of the potential earlier forts' base.

The village is charming and you can catch a bus to Carlisle from here, or the AD 122 Hadrian's Wall service. Do take time to explore – the views over the Solway are a delight and the village has spent much time and effort restoring 'Solway Banks', a lovely little public garden which delights in celebrating Bowness-on-Solway's Hadrianic connection. There is a Roman-style shelter with a mosaic floor designed by the children of Bowness-on-Solway Primary School. It shows some of the wildlife and makes a very attractive spot to stop momentarily and take in the view. Closer to the water's edge is a substantial bench designed with a back like a haff net, the traditional and nearly extinct

Solway Firth fishing net. All these good works were a combination of locals getting together and funding from the local Heritage Initiative, which is administered locally via the Solway Discovery Centre offices.

The King's Arms provides thirst-quenching beverages, sustenance and the chance of a bed for the night. Book well in advance for this most popular of establishments – a warm welcome is assured.

Go and get your feet wet. I hope you have found this a most enjoyable trip with plenty of contrasting scenery, good food and decent people along the way. Well done! You have made it! Of course, you could continue to Wallsend should you so wish, but perhaps that is for another day?

The author is off to start the Roman Ravenglass to Ambleside walking guide and hopes you will enjoy that one too. May all your journeys be prosperous!

FACILITIES: ABBEYTOWN TO BOWNESS-ON-SOLWAY

Bowness-on-Solway

Restaurants, pubs, hotels, B&B
Kings Arms: Just what you need after a long journey. A relaxing, friendly spot. Good food, beer and rooms.
The Old Chapel: B&B.

Other attractions
The Solway Banks garden: a joy.

Other facilities
Post Office.
Bus service to Carlisle.

Far left: *Pint anyone? Bowness-on-Solway.*

Left: *Where shall we go next?*

DAY 9

General Information

TRANSPORT

Traveline
08706 082608

National Rail Enquiries
http://www.nationalrail.co.uk/
Tel: 08457 484950

Northern Rail
http://www.northernrail.org/
Barrow-in-Furness to Carlisle
– The Cumbrian Coastline (including
Ravenglass & Eskdale Railway),
Timetable 6

General Customer Helpline
(for comments/complaints/queries)
customer.relations@northernrail.org
Tel: 0845 000 0125

Telesales & Bookings
Tel: 0845 700 0125

**Access/Disabled Information
& Cycle Assistance**
assistance@northernrail.org
Tel: 0845 600 8008

Lost Property
lost.property@northernrail.org
Tel: 0870 602 3322

Railway stations en route
Ravenglass for Eskdale (No Service Sunday)

Drigg	As above
Seascale	As above
Sellafield	As above
Nethertown	As above
Braystones	As above
St Bees	As above

Whitehaven Bransty
Parton
Harrington
Workington
Flimby
Maryport
Aspatria (Not en route but useful for Silloth)
Wigton (Not en route but useful for Bowness-on-Solway)

Stagecoach North West
http://www.stagecoachbus.com/
northwest/index.html
Tel: 01228 597222

Journeyplanner North East & Cumbria
http://www.traveline.info/index.htm

Ravenglass & Eskdale Railway
Tel: 01229 717171

Cumbria Tourism
http://www.golakes.co.uk/

Gosforth Taxis (for Wasdale Link)
Tel: 019467 25308

Whitehaven taxis

Wilson's of Whitehaven	01946 692269
Brian's Taxis	01946 690444
RTS Services	01946 694455
White Line Taxis	01946 66111
L&G	01946 66644
Bee-Line	01946 691111
KLM Cabs	01946 66007
A2B Taxis	01946 599407
Ajax Cab Co	01946 695000
KLM Cabs	01946 66585
Call A Cab	01946 691415
Abbey Cabs	01946 63000
S&L Cabs	01946 64205
Ding Dongs	01946 66666

Workington taxis

Cable Cars	01900 601122
B Cabs	01900 65968
Lynda's Taxis	01900 870945
Syd's	01900 605405
Sue's	01900 607005
A&G Taxis	01900 62469
Joe's	01900 66899
J&E Taxis	01900 603713
Sparky's	01900 601999

Maryport taxis

Waffy's Private Hire	01900 819641
Cooter's Cabs	01900 814141
Geoff's	01900 816767

Silloth Taxi   **01697 331508**

MEDICAL

Hospitals

West Cumberland Hospital
Hensingham, Whitehaven
Cumbria CA28 8JG
http://www.cumbria.nhs.uk/acute/
hospitals/wch.aspx
Tel: 01946 693181

Cumberland Infirmary
Newtown Road, Carlisle
Cumbria CA2 7HY
http://www.cumbria.nhs.uk/acute/
hospitals/cic.aspx
Tel: 01228 523444

Health Centres

Seascale Health Centre
Gosforth Road, Seascale,
Cumbria CA20 1PN
Tel: 01946 728101

Flatt Walks Medical Centre
3 Castle Meadows, Whitehaven
Cumbria, CA28 7QE
Tel. 01946 692173

Workington Health Centre
South William Street, Workington
Cumbria CA14 2ED
Tel: 01900 603985

Maryport Health Services
Alneburgh House
Ewanrigg Road Maryport
Cumbria CA15 8EL
Tel: 01900 815544

Silloth Group Medical Practice
Lawn Terrace
Silloth, Wigton
Cumbria CA7 4AH
Tel: 016973 31309

The Croft Surgery
Kirkbride, Wigton
Cumbria, CA7 5JH
Tel: 016973 51207

Pharmacists

Seascale Pharmacy Ltd.
Gosforth Road, Seascale,
Cumbria, CA20 1PR
Tel: 019467 28323

Tesco Instore Pharmacy
Bransty Row,
North Shore, Whitehaven,
Cumbria CA28 7XY
Tel: 01946 852449

Boots the Chemist
26 King Street, Whitehaven,
Cumbria CA28 7JN
Tel: 01946 692042

Boots the Chemist
29 Murray Road, Workington,
Cumbria CA14 2AB
Tel: 01900 602405

H.S. Dobie Chemists Ltd
29 Curzon Street, Maryport,
Cumbria CA15 6LN
Tel: 01900 812662

Bowmans Chemist (Carlisle) Ltd
1-3 Station Road, Silloth,
Cumbria CA7 4AE
Tel: 016973 31394

EMERGENCY SERVICES

Police, Fire, Ambulance, Coastguard

Dial 999
When asked for your location, in rural locations give a map reference. For the deaf and hearing and speech impaired, send a text message. Text where you are and why you need help to: 07786 208999

Police
Non-emergency number:
0845 33 00 247

Police Stations
Whitehaven, Scotch Street
Whitehaven CA28 7NN
This station is manned
8 a.m. to 12 midnight

Workington
Hall Brow, Workington CA14 4AP
This station is manned
8 a.m. to 12 midnight

Maryport
Eaglesfield Street, Maryport CA15 6HG
This station is manned
9 a.m. to 5 p.m., Monday-Friday

Wigton
Station Road , Wigton CA7 9AH
This station is manned between
9 a.m.-5 p.m., Monday-Friday

WEATHER

Met Office: St Bees Head
http://www.metoffice.gov.uk/weather/uk/
nw/st_bees_head_latest_weather.html

LOCAL RADIO

CFM
http://www.cfmradio.com/

**Carlisle and Southwest Scotland
96.4 FM**
Workington - 102.2 FM
Whitehaven - 103.4 FM

BBC Radio Cumbria
http://www.bbc.co.uk/cumbria/local_radio/

Frequency: North, East and West
95.6 FM
South 96.1 FM
Whitehaven 104.1 FM

BOOT REPAIRS

Timpson Shoe Repairs Ltd
23 Pow Street, Workington,
Cumbria, CA14 3AG
Tel: 01900 603087

Timpson Shoe Repairs Ltd
79a King Street, Whitehaven,
Cumbria CA28 7LE
Tel: 01946 692444

A SELECTION OF HOTELS, PUBS & ATTRACTIONS ALONG THE ROUTE – NOT A DEFINITIVE LIST

Ravenglass

The Pennington	01229 717222
The Ratty Arms	01229 717676
Holly House	01229 717230
Rosegarth	01229 717275
Walls Caravan Park	01229 717250
Muncaster Guest House	01229 717693
The Old Butcher's Shop	01229 717273

Saltcoats

Saltcoats Caravan Park	01229 717241

Drigg

The Victoria Hotel	01946 724231
Spindle Craft (shop)	01946 724335

Seascale

The Calder House Hotel	01946 728538
The Cumbrian Lodge	01946 727309
Eskdale House	019467 28619
Wansfell	01946 728314

Beckermet

The White Mare	01946 841246
Royal Oak Hotel	01946 841551

St Bees

Platform 9	01946 822600
Fleatham House	01946 822341
Tomlin Guest House	01946 822284
Manor House	01946 822425
Stonehouse Farm	01946 822224
Fairladies Barn	01946 822718

Whitehaven

Glenfield House	01946 691911
Chase Hotel	01946 693656
The Waverley Hotel	01946 694337
The Rum Story	01946 592933
Espresso Café	01946 591548
Akash Tandoori	01946 691171
Ali Taj	01946 693085
Blue	01946 691986
Casa Romana	01946 591901
Crosby Seafood Restaurant	01946 62622
Zest	01946 692848

Moresby

Moresby Hall	01946 696317

Harrington

Riversleigh Guest House	01946 830267

Workington

Fernleigh House	01900 605811
Hall Park Hotel	01900 602968
Morven House	01900 602118
Washington Central Hotel	01900 65772

Maryport

Riverside B&B	01900 813595
Harbourside Guest House	01900 815137
Shore Walk Guest House	01900 810085
Waverley Hotel	01900 812115

Allonby

The Ship Inn	01900 881017
Baywatch Hotel	01946 822345

Silloth-on-Solway

Nith View Guest House	016973 32860
West View Guest House	016973 31449

Golf Hotel	01697 331438
Winters, Eden Street (Post Office) Solway Discovery Centre	01697 333055

Abbeytown

Wheyrigg Hall Farmhouse Hotel	01697 361242
Wheatsheaf Inn	01697 361317

Newton Arlosh

Joiner's Arms Country Inn	01697 351470

Kirkbride

Bush Inn	01697 351694

Bowness-on-Solway

King's Arms	01697 351426
The Old Chapel B&B	01697 351126

Bibliography

Bellhouse, R., *Roman Sites on the Cumberland Coast: A new schedule of coastal sites*, Cumberland & Westmorland Antiquarian & Archaeological Society Research Series, Volume III (1989)

Hanson, W.S., and Keppie, L.J.F., *Frontier Studies*, Oxford (1979)

Higham, N.J. and Jones, G.D.B, 'Frontier, forts and farmers. Cumbria aerial survey 1974-75'. in *Archaeological Journal* 132: 16-53 (1975)

Potter T., *Romans in North West England* (1979)

Wilson, J., 'Houses of Benedictine Monks: The Priory of St Bees', in *The Victoria History of the County of Cumberland: Vol.2*, Victoria County History (1905)

Zeller Van P., Ravenglass: Roman Port to Railway Junction (2001)

ORGANISATIONS (TO WHOM GRATEFUL THANKS ARE GIVEN)

Durham Mining Museum
c/o Thornley Community Centre, Hartlepool Street,
Thornley, Co. Durham DH6 3AB

Pits & Workings: Whitehaven and Workington environs

Cumbria Railway Association
c/oThe Membership Secretary, 36 Clevelands Avenue,
Barrow in Furness, Cumbria LA13 0AE

Railways of West Cumbria

Workington Civic Trust
c/o The Membership Secretary, 34 Dora Crescent, Workington CA14 2EZ

History of Workington

Natural England
Juniper House, Murley Moss, Oxenholme Rd, Kendal, Cumbria LA9 7RL

West Cumbrian coast habitats

English Heritage
Canada House, 3 Chepstow Street, Manchester M1 5FW

Archaeological Sites Cumbrian coast

Solway Discovery Centre
Liddell Street, Silloth-on-Solway, Cumbria CA7 4DD

AONB Solway centre

RSPB
The Lodge, Sandy, Bedfordshire, SG19 2DL

Birds of the Cumbrian Coast

Cumbria Wildlife Trust
Plumgarth, Crook Road, Kendal, Cumbria LA8 8LX

Wildlife of the Cumbrian Coast

Hadrian's Wall Heritage Ltd
East Peterel Field, Dipton Mill road, Hexham, Northumberland NE46 2JT

Promotion of better facilities for visitors
Community archaeology

Hadrian's Wall Country
http://www.hadrians-wall.org/

Portal to details of Hadrian's Wall, including Western Frontier

British Museum
http://www.thebritishmuseum.ac.uk/explore/highlights/highlight_objects/
pe_prb/w/writing-tablet_with_an_intelli.aspx

National Health Service
http://www.nhs.uk/Pages/homepage.aspx

Cumbria Constabulary

If you are interested in purchasing other books published by Tempus, or in case you have difficulty finding any Tempus books in your local bookshop, you can also place orders directly through our website

www.thehistorypress.co.uk